UNIFORMS OF THE
AMERICAN REVOLUTION

UNIFORMS OF THE
AMERICAN REVOLUTION

JOHN MOLLO

Illustrated by Malcolm McGregor

BLANDFORD PRESS
POOLE · DORSET

First published in the U.K. 1975
by Blandford Press, Link House, West Street,
Poole, Dorset BH15 1LL

Copyright © 1975 Blandford Press Ltd.
Reprinted in paperback 1985

Distributed in the United States by
Sterling Publishing Co., Inc.,
2 Park Avenue, New York, N.Y. 10016

ISBN 0 7137 1603 7

Printed in Hong Kong by
South China Printing Co.

CONTENTS

PREFACE

In this book Malcolm McGregor and I have attempted to recreate the appearance of those taking part in the turbulent events which surrounded the birth of the United States of America, 200 years ago. In order to add realism to our impression of the period, we have drawn freely on contemporary civilian and military portraits. This explains the appearance of many people in this book who will seem familiar to the reader from less warlike surroundings.

One of the biggest problems of our work has been the lack of reliable source material, particularly in the case of the American combatants. It is perhaps not surprising that, in the middle of fighting a revolution, the Americans failed to record for posterity the details of their clothing. In the case of the other contestants however – the British, the Germans, and the French, who were supposedly dressed according to surviving written regulations – it is remarkable how many gaps there are in our knowledge of their appearance, and how much of what we do know is contradictory.

As in all military uniform research the sources are varied, drawn mainly from examples, combined with pictorial and written material. The number of genuine relics which have survived from the period is extremely few. Unless some new cache of pictures is discovered, the pictorial sources, which are also few in number, have been exhaustively researched and examined. Apart from numerous portraits of Washington and his generals, and Trumbull's epic pieces painted some years after the war, we have little contemporary American material beyond a few sketches of the Saratoga and Yorktown campaigns, both done by foreigners.

For the British uniforms we have numerous portraits of officers, De Loutherbourg's paintings of the Siege of Gibraltar and Warley Camp, the preparatory sketches for the latter, the paintings and drawings of British troops in Minorca by an unknown hand, the series of watercolours of Grenadiers in the Prince Consort's Library, Aldershot, and perhaps most important of all, two small *gouache* paintings by an Italian, Xavier Gatta, showing British troops in America in a campaign dress not shown anywhere else. For the French there are portraits, watercolours and prints, and for the Germans a few stiff little engravings. The written material in the case of the Americans consists largely of advertisements for deserters in the newspapers of the time, and returns of yardages of cloth and other equipment issued to the regiments of the Continental army from time to time.

The basic source book for the uniforms of the American revolution was compiled posthumously from the notes of Lieutenant Charles M. Lefferts who spent a lifetime examining and collecting what information was then available on the subject. Working largely from the mass of deserter descriptions, Lefferts reconstructed a series of plates of the participants, but much of his information remains in note form. Since his death in 1923 students have questioned some of his findings and have unearthed new information, the bulk of which can be found in the pages of the *Military Collector and Historian*, the journal of the Company of Military Historians, published in the United States. This new material has been carefully examined and the relevant information has been included. Much research remains to be done, however, such as sifting through clothing returns in the archives of the various states, and examining letters and other documents tucked away in archives all over the world.

From these diverse sources we have thus been able to present a wider range of reconstructed uniforms than has appeared before in one volume. On occasion we have used our knowledge of the general costume of the period to complete a figure, but wherever possible our sources have been quoted.

A few additional comments may be helpful to the reader. A few British and American 'Orders of Battle' have been included at various points in the text. These are intended purely as indications of how the various armies were organised at a given moment, and should not be taken as rigid formations which lasted for any length of time. The figures for the strengths of the various forces, where given, are drawn from a wide variety of sources, and are intended only as a rough guide. Finally, the absence of any Spanish uniforms may be noted. These have not been included because of the small number of units serving in North America and because their actions took place very much on the side-lines.

My chief acknowledgement is due to Malcolm McGregor for the patience and skill with which he has transformed a mass of complicated notes into such a magnificent array of warriors. For other help I must express my thanks to the directors and staffs of the National Army Museum, London, the Victoria and Albert Museum Library, London, the National Maritime Museum,

Greenwich, the Musée de la Marine, Paris, the Musée de l'Armée, Paris, M. Jean Brunon and, as always, for their help and criticism, my brothers Boris and Andrew. Lastly our thanks must go to all the authors and artists, from Lefferts to the present day, without whose painstaking work, this book would not have been possible. Space will not permit me to mention them all by name, but I have listed those to whom I am most indebted in the Bibliography at the end.

London, 1974.   J.M.

THE BRITISH ARMY

When the American revolution broke out in April 1775 the bulk of the British army, considerably reduced after the Seven Years War, was distributed in three main areas. Disregarding the militia, there were 15,000 troops in England, 12,000 in Ireland, and 8,000 in North America. The remaining 10,000 were scattered among the garrisons in the West Indies, Africa, Minorca, Gibraltar and Scotland.

The regiments that composed this army were of two kinds, the Household troops, and the regiments of the line. The former consisted of two troops of Horse Guards, two troops of Horse Grenadier Guards, the Royal Regiment of Horse Guards, and the three regiments of Foot Guards, the First, the Coldstream and the Third. The regiments of the line were simply the ordinary regiments of the army and consisted of four regiments of Horse, three regiments of Dragoon Guards, thirteen regiments of Dragoons, and five regiments of Light Dragoons. There were seventy regiments of infantry numbered 1–70.

The average strength of an infantry regiment on the English establishment was 477, consisting of one battalion divided into ten companies, one of which was a 'grenadier' company, and another a 'light infantry' company. When introduced at the end of the previous century, the rôle of the grenadiers had been to hurl hand grenades at the enemy from close range, a task calling for a strong physique. By 1775 the grenades had disappeared but the grenadiers remained, representing in height and strength the cream of each regiment.

Light infantry had been tried out in North America during the French and Indian wars, and were introduced throughout the army in 1771. Good marksmen, of light build and active temperament, were chosen for this service, providing each regiment with its own corps of skirmishers. The grenadiers and light infantry together represented the picked men of a regiment, and from their position on the right and left flanks respectively, became known as the 'flank companies' in contrast to their less-gifted comrades merely known as 'hatmen'. When a large force assembled it was customary to form the flank companies into one or two special battalions, to unite their strength and skills for the many occasions when they were called upon to display both. The remaining companies, known collectively as the 'battalion companies', were trained to move and fight in line and in column, to march and wheel in exact cadence, to handle their arms correctly and smartly, and to load and fire as nimbly as possible. The platoon firing of the British infantry, like that of their late German allies, was renowned throughout Europe and most armies, including the French, tried to emulate it.

The cavalry consisted of two kinds, heavy and light. The former comprised Horse, Dragoon Guards, and Dragoons, and the latter Light Dragoons, who were an élite corps priding themselves on their weapon handling and horsemanship. Only two regiments served in America, the 16th and 17th, although there were numerous irregular units of a similar nature. The normal establishment was 231 men formed into six troops.

At the outbreak of the war the Royal Regiment of Artillery consisted of four battalions of eight or more companies each, the 4th Battalion providing the bulk of those who served in America, although the 1st and 3rd Battalions were also represented. They were supplied with guns at a rate which was to hold good from the days of Cromwell to the Second World War, namely three pieces for every 1,000 men. The customary system of allocating two 'battalion guns' to each infantry regiment was going out of fashion, and both Howe and Burgoyne divided their artillery into 'brigades', one assigned to the centre of the line and one to each of the flanks. In Burgoyne's case each brigade consisted of a battery of four 6-pounders.

At the time of the American revolution the staff organisation of the British army was of a very rudimentary nature. Two, three, or four battalions were formed into brigades, under a major- or brigadier-general, and two or more brigades might be formed into divisions. Each general officer had the assistance of one or more aides-de-camp, and those commanding brigades might have extra assistance in the form of a brigade-major. The commander-in-chief might also have a military secretary. The staff was only organised in time of war, and its two most important administrators were the quartermaster-general and the adjutant-general. The former dealt with matters of organisation, operations, transport and supply. He also regulated all marches, furnished maps, and provided guides.

The adjutant-general received the instructions of the commander-in-chief, direct or from the major-general of the day, and issued the necessary orders to regimental adjutants through the channel of the brigade-major.

At the beginning of a campaign the quartermaster-general drew up the 'Order of Battle' in accordance with which the army encamped and formed for battle. The army was usually formed in two lines divided into two wings, each commanded by a major-general, with the senior brigade taking the right of the front line. The organisation of the order of battle, and the allocation of the flank positions or 'posts of honour', exercised much of the quartermaster-general's time and tact in appeasing military jealousies. The brigades were formed by dealing out the regiments like cards in the following order: right, left, right centre, left centre. So the senior regiment would be posted on the right of the line and the next senior on the left. Within the brigade the senior regiment would take the right, the next the left, and the next the centre positions, a system which still holds good among the regiments of foot guards in the British army. The artillery was usually posted in the front line, and the cavalry on either flank, and if there were rifles or other light troops with the army they were placed in front or on either flank.

The standard weapon of the British infantryman was the smooth-bore flintlock musket, known as 'Brown Bess', which had been in use since 1717. It weighed 6 kg (14 lb) had a barrel either 106 cm or 117 cm long (42 in. or 46 in.), and fired a round lead ball weighing roughly an ounce, made up, with its charge of powder, into a stout paper cartridge. With its sporting stock, well-shaped brass furniture, and lock which had the reputation of misfiring less often than any other military firearm, it was eminently suited to the close-order, short-range, volley firing of the day. Of its accuracy, Colonel Hanger, who served in America with the Hessian Jägers and Tarleton's Legion, had this to say:

> A soldier's musket, if not exceedingly ill-bored, (as many are), will strike the figure of a man at 80 yards; it may be even at a hundred; but a soldier must be very unfortunate indeed who shall be wounded by a common musket at 150 yards, provided his antagonist aims at him; and as to firing at a man at 200 yards with a common musket, you may as well fire at the moon . . .

Although twelve separate motions were required to prime and load flintlock muskets, a well-trained soldier could load and fire five times a minute. Nevertheless this type of weapon had one very serious drawback; its efficiency was largely dependent on the weather. A high wind might blow the priming out of the pan, or a rainstorm might wash it out, or dampen it so that it would not ignite. Prolonged rain might soak through the ammunition pouch, or 'cartouche box', and turn the cartridges into a pulp. Perhaps because of this unreliability officers trained in the school of European warfare placed great reliance on the bayonet. After the first battle of Freeman's Farm, Burgoyne, while complimenting his men on their gallantry, also had occasion to complain of the mistake they were still committing 'in preferring firing to the bayonet'. Grenadiers were armed with muskets, bayonets and hangers, or short swords, and the light infantry with shortened muskets, bayonets and tomahawks. Sergeants carried swords and halberds, and officers swords and espontoons, or half-pikes, but gradually both these ranks copied the light infantry and adopted fusils and bayonets. The artillery were also armed with light muskets and bayonets. The light dragoons carried flintlock carbines, with 74 cm (29 in.) barrels, a pair of pistols with 23 cm (9 in.) barrels, and a sword, 'either crooked or straight according to the regulations of the Regiment'.

The British army entered the war with no rifles of any description but soon acquired the best and most revolutionary model in the world, invented by Captain Patrick Ferguson of the 71st Highlanders. It was a breech-loader with an ingenious loading mechanism that gave it a rate of fire faster than a smoothbore. It had a 89 cm (35 in.) barrel and, unlike other rifles, was equipped with sword-bayonet with a flat single-edge blade 65 cm (25½ in.) long. In June 1776 Ferguson gave a demonstration of his weapon at Woolwich during which in spite of high wind and heavy rain he fired for five minutes at the rate of four shots a minute at a target 200 yards away.

The guns of the artillery fell into two categories, field and siege artillery. The field artillery, along with other ordnance, had been greatly improved from 1755 onwards through the efforts of John Müller, principal of the Royal Military Academy at Woolwich. The field guns in common use were brass 3-pounders and 6-pounders, although 12-pounders and even larger guns were used on occasion. The problem of transportation however, was the main limiting factor.

A 6-pounder complete with carriage weighed between 385 and 544 kg (850 and 1,200 lb), which was about as much as two wheels could carry on colonial roads, but the 3-pounder, at 317 kg (700 lb), could be manhandled with ease by four men. There were special light 3-pounders, mounted on 'Congreve' carriages, which could be carried on pack animals.

The gun carriages were usually of the Müller 'bracket trail' variety with 130 cm (51 in.) diameter wheels. The limbers consisted of another pair of wheels with shafts for one horse, additional horses being hitched in front in tandem. In Burgoyne's army of 1777, a 6-pounder was drawn by four horses, and a 3-pounder and a 'Royal' howitzer, by three. There were also 'Galloper' guns, or light pieces mounted on split trail carriages, the trails of which were stout enough to withstand the shock of firing and to act as two shafts for a horse. While the gunners and mattrosses were enlisted men, the horses and wagons (obtained by hire or impressment) were usually civilians, although the Royal Artillery did have some drafts of trained drivers sent out to America.

The projectile most commonly used was a solid shot, canister being used only in emergency situations. Howitzers fired shell in limited quantities. The charges for field pieces were put up in cylindrical cloth bags. A small supply of ammunition was carried in axletree boxes on either side of the piece, and additional supplies were carried in tumbrils, carts and wagons, usually drawn by three horses. The greatest effective range of field guns was under 1,000 yards (914 m) with solid shot, and even less with canister. When the guns were manoeuvred in action by the gunners it was done by means of handspikes and drag-ropes.

Siege and garrison artillery, used for reducing or defending fortified places, consisted of 18- and 24-pounder guns, and larger varieties of howitzers and mortars.

The uniform of the infantry consisted of a black felt hat, adorned with a black 'military' or Hanoverian cockade, the familiar red coat, with different colour facings and laced button-holes for each regiment, waistcoat, breeches, gaiters and shoes. The co-operation with the Prussians during the Seven Years War had resulted in 1768 in a drastic change in the style of these clothes. The hat became less of a three-cornered hat and more of a cocked hat, and the coat was made less voluminous and was furnished with a collar, long narrow lapels, and small round cuffs. The waistcoats and breeches, formerly red, were changed to white on the grounds that they were easier to keep clean. The black marching gaiters, and the white dress gaiters, both of which reached up to above the knee, were retained for the time being. The infantryman's equipment consisted of a leather waist-belt which supported his bayonet and hanger, and a stout leather cartouche box holding sixty rounds of ammunition hung from a leather belt worn over the left shoulder.

Officers wore uniforms (of a better quality) which were superficially the same as those of their men. Although epaulettes had recently been introduced in place of the old-fashioned shoulder-cords, there were as yet no distinguishing rank badges, and the chief distinction of an officer was the wearing of a gorget at the throat and a crimson sash round the waist.

Highland national dress was worn by certain regiments recruited in Scotland. Their coats were shorter, more in the style of a jacket, and in place of hats and breeches, they wore Scots bonnets, belted plaids, and diced hose. Their waist- and bayonet-belts were of black leather.

On service or on the march, the infantryman carried extra clothing and cleaning materials, Indian fashion, in a knapsack in the middle of his back, supported by two leather straps over his shoulders and under the armpits. In addition he carried a blanket, a haversack with provisions, a canteen of water, and a fifth share of the general equipment belonging to his tent. With provisions for four days and sixty rounds of ammunition, and his arms, this burden was estimated to weigh in the order of 27 kg (60 lb).

Grenadiers wore special caps, which had been changed in 1768 from cloth 'mitre' caps with embroidered fronts to fur caps with a metal plate in front. The shoulders of their coats were ornamented with 'wings', and they carried match-cases, relics of their former duties, on their cartouche box-belts. The light infantry developed a distinctive style of dress based on the custom, started by General Wolfe in Canada, of cutting the brims off their hats to make caps, and taking the sleeves off their coats, which they cut short, and attaching them to their waistcoats. When light companies were reintroduced in 1771 they wore a variety of small caps, short jackets with wings on the shoulders, red waistcoats, white breeches and stockings, and calf-length 'half-spatterdashes'.

The general wear and tear of campaigning, together with the difficulty of keeping up supplies of new clothing, led to a change in the appearance of the British army from the smartness and pipeclay to be seen in the Boston Garrison of 1775. Unfortunately there is all too little detailed information about this change. Apart from two watercolours, by Xavier Gatta, which show the use of wide-brimmed 'slouch' hats, sleeved red waistcoats and one-piece canvas gaiter-overalls, we have only the evidence of a set of drawings by v. Germann which show the regiments of Burgoyne's army in crested light infantry caps, and short jackets. The very interesting set of oil-paintings of the 25th Regiment at Minorca of a slightly earlier period show how articles of the earlier period were still worn side-by-side with the new. They also show, as does Morier in his paintings at Windsor, how the custom of wearing the waist-belt over the right shoulder, for convenience's sake, gradually brought about a change to a proper shoulder bayonet-belt with a plate to keep it in position with the cartouche box-belt.

The light dragoons were dressed in red like the infantry, with special caps, boots and spurs. Their swords were worn either on a waist-belt or shoulder-belt over the right shoulder, and their carbines were suspended from another shoulder-belt over the left shoulder, which also carried a pouch containing twenty-four rounds. The artillery were dressed like the line infantry but in blue with red facings and yellow lace.

The outbreak of the American revolution and the need for extra troops drew attention to the serious recruiting problem that existed, partly caused by the soldiers' pay of 8d per day. After the usual deductions had been made from it, this left him with hardly enough to exist on, let alone enjoy any recreation which might cost money. According to one officer, common toilers were far better off than soldiers, and a tailor, weaver, or mechanic, could live on his wages more respectably than an officer. There was little honour attached to the military life; there were no medals and decorations; indeed, the soldier was either ridiculed by the public, or regarded as the natural enemy of the liberties of the people. Such were the difficulties of persuading people to enlist that officers were loth to part with old soldiers, however inefficient, as long as they could walk, and the undesirable and illegal recruiting in Leinster, Munster, and Connaught was openly practised. Between the outbreak of the war and the disaster of Saratoga, only one regiment, the 71st, was raised, so that it is hardly surprising that the government was prepared not only to enlist foreigners in British regiments, but to seek the services of the Scots Brigade in Holland, the armies of the petty German princelings, or even of Catherine the Great of Russia.

With the news of Saratoga the situation changed dramatically. The loss of 4,000 troops serving in America as the terms of the surrender demanded, was not irreparable, and there were certain compensations like the destruction of much American material and the recapture of Fort Ticonderoga. Nevertheless a regular British army had been beaten and captured, a serious blow to Britain's reputation, and encouragement was given to the rebels.

Within a few months Britain and France were at war, and fear of an imminent invasion, coupled with a revision of the recruiting laws, greatly improved the recruiting figures. In the spring of 1778 no less than twelve new regiments, numbered 72-83, were raised, to be followed in the spring of 1779 by the 84th and three regiments of light dragoons, 19th–21st. The declaration of war with Spain that year led to further activity. In the summer and autumn thirteen regiments of foot, 85th–97th, and one of light dragoons, the 22nd, were raised, with three more infantry regiments, 98th–100th, the following winter. Adding to these two more regiments, the 101st and 102nd which appeared in the Army List for 1781, and not counting irregular formations, no fewer than thirty-one independent regiments of foot, and four of light dragoons, were created between 1778 and 1781. The 48,000 troops of 1775 had increased to 110,000 of which some 56,000 were in America, not allowing for the thousands who died from sickness or the accidents of war. The new regiments were mostly disbanded at the end of the war in 1783.

The failure of British arms in America cannot be ascribed to want of courage or training on the part of the officers and men. Lexington came as a revelation, and Bunker Hill as confirmation that the subjugation of the colonies would not be child's play, but throughout the war the British were almost invariably successful in pitched battles. The disasters at Saratoga and Yorktown were due less to the qualities of the British troops involved, than to lack of supplies and bad planning in one case, and bad planning and appalling naval and military co-operation in the other.

Two years after Saratoga a small British force, composed entirely of veterans from America under a good general, were able to beat decisively a larger number of French troops, which were then perhaps the best trained and organised forces in Europe, and to repulse them from St Lucia.

The failure has often been attributed to inept leadership, at sea as much as on land, but the negligence, corruption, and inefficiency of the army's administration, combined with the natural obstacles of the country were as much to blame. The British, separated from their home base by over 3,000 miles of sea, across which all their supplies had to be transported, had to cover great distances over poor roads, through a countryside too sparsely populated to supply their needs. Unlike Europe, there were no large fortified towns to be captured as a means of imposing control over a wide area. Military efficiency was practically unknown at the time of Germain and North, so that the chances of a military success were correspondingly reduced to a minimum. As one historian has summed it up:

> Divided authority, interdepartmental friction, clumsy methods of business, ignorance and incompetence had characterized the rule of the mother country from the foundation of the colonies. The ineptitude displayed by the home government in military affairs during the American Revolution may thus be viewed merely as another manifestation of a long-standing evil.

List of British Troops Serving in North America, *1775–1783*

Regiment or Corps	Period of Service	Chief Incidents
1st Foot Guards ⎫ Coldstream Guards ⎬ 3rd Foot Guards ⎭	1776–1783	Brooklyn, New York, Brandywine, Germantown, Guildford Courthouse, Yorktown.
3rd, or the Buffs	1781–1782	S. Carolina.
4th, or the King's Own	1775–1778	Lexington, Bunker Hill, Brooklyn, New York, Germantown.
5th	1774–1778	Lexington, Bunker Hill, Brooklyn, Bronx, Brandywine, Germantown.

Regiment or Corps	*Period of* *Service*	Chief Incidents
6th	1776	
7th, or Royal Fusiliers	1774–1783	Quebec, Bronz, the Carolinas.
8th, or King's	1768–1785	Quebec.
9th	1777–1781	Saratoga.
10th	1774–1778	Lexington, Bunker Hill, Brooklyn, Bronx, Brandywine, Germantown.
14th	1768–1777	
15th	1776–1778	Charleston, Brooklyn, New York, Brandywine, Germantown, Freehold, Florida.
16th	1768–1782	Florida, the Carolinas.
17th	1775–1783	Brooklyn, New York, Brandywine, Germantown, Stony Point, Freehold, Yorktown.
18th	1768–1776	Lexington, Bunker Hill.
19th	1781–1782	The Carolinas, Eutaw Springs.
20th	1776–1781	Saratoga.
21st, or Royal North British Fusiliers	1776–1781	Saratoga.
22nd	1775–1783	Bunker Hill, Brooklyn, New York, Rhode Island.
23rd, or Royal Welch Fusiliers	1773–1783	Lexington, Bunker Hill, Brooklyn, New York, Brandywine, service as Marines 1779, Camden, Yorktown.
24th	1776–1781	Saratoga.
26th	1767–1779	Canada, Brooklyn, New York, the Carolinas.
27th, or Inniskilling		
28th	1776–1778	Canada, Brooklyn, New York, Florida

Regiment or Corps	Period of Service	Chief Incidents
29th	1777–1781	Saratoga.
30th	1781–1783	The Carolinas.
31st	1776–1781	Saratoga.
33rd	1776–1782	Charleston, Brooklyn, New York, Fort Washington, Brandywine, Guildford Courthouse, Camden, Yorktown.
34th	1776–1781	Saratoga.
35th	1775–1778	Bunker Hill, Brooklyn, New York.
37th	1776–1783	Charleston, Brooklyn, New York, Brandywine.
38th	1774–1783	Lexington, Bunker Hill, Brooklyn, New York.
40th	1775–1778	Brooklyn, New York, Brandywine, Germantown, Florida.
42nd, or Royal Highland	1776–1783	Brooklyn, New York, Fort Washington, Brandywine, Germantown, Freehold, Florida, Halifax.
43rd	1774–1783	Lexington, Bunker Hill, Brooklyn, New York, Rhode Island, Florida, Yorktown.
44th	1775–1780	Brooklyn, New York, Brandywine, Freehold.
45th	1775–1778	Brooklyn, New York.
46th	1774–1778	Charleston, Brooklyn, New York, Brandywine, Florida.
47th	1774–1781	Lexington, Bunker Hill, Saratoga.
49th	1775–1778	Bunker Hill, Brooklyn, New York, Brandywine, Florida.

Regiment or Corps	Period of Service	Chief Incidents
50th	1776	
52nd	1774–1778	Lexington, Bunker Hill, Brandywine, Freehold.
53rd	1776–1781	Saratoga.
54th	1776–1782	Charleston, Brooklyn, New York, Rhode Island.
55th	1775–1778	Brooklyn, Brandywine, Germantown, Florida.
57th	1776–1783	Charleston, Brooklyn, New York, the Carolinas.
59th	1774–1775	Lexington, Bunker Hill.
60th, or Royal American	1778–1783	Charleston, New York, Halifax.
62nd	1776–1781	Saratoga.
63rd	1775–1782	Bunker Hill, Brooklyn, New York, Brandywine, Germantown, the Carolinas.
64th	1773–1782	Bunker Hill, Brooklyn, New York, Brandywine, the Carolinas.
65th	1774–1776	Bunker Hill, Charleston.
70th	1779–1782	The Carolinas (flank companies only).
71st, Highland (Fraser's)	1776–1783	Brooklyn, Brandywine, the Carolinas.
74th	1779–1783	
76th, Highlanders (Macdonalds)	1779–1783	The Carolinas, Yorktown.
80th, or Royal Edinburgh Volunteers	1778–1783	Yorktown.
82nd (2nd Bn. 84th)	1778–1783	
84th, or Royal Highland Emigrants	1779–1783	Camden, The Carolinas, New York.
105th, or Volunteers of Ireland		
Marines	1774–1783	Lexington, Bunker Hill.

Regiment or Corps	Period of Service	Chief Incidents
16th, or the Queen's Light Dragoons	1776–1778	Home after Monmouth.
17th Light Dragoons	1775–1783	
1st Bn. Royal Artillery, 1st Coy.		
3rd Bn. Royal Artillery, 1st Coy.		Charleston, Guildford Courthouse.
3rd Bn. Royal Artillery, 6th Coy.		Charleston.
4th Bn. Royal Artillery, 1st–5th and 8th Coys.		Bunker Hill, Brooklyn, New York, Brandywine, Freehold, Savannah, Charleston.

2

GERMAN AUXILIARY TROOPS

We have seen that the events of 1775 and the need for large reinforcements in North America exposed the weakness of the British
army, but even so it was not until August of that year that the
establishment was increased from 33,000 to 55,000 men, and this
was on paper only, for recruits were extremely difficult to acquire.
In this crisis the British government turned to Catherine II of
Russia for a loan of 20,000 men, but, persuaded by Frederick the
Great, she refused to help. The next potential source of recruits was
Germany, and, as Elector of Hanover, George III first made himself
a loan of five Hanoverian battalions, which were sent to Gibraltar
and Minorca to relieve the same number of British battalions. On
hearing the news of Bunker Hill, three of the three hundred or so
petty German princes offered military aid to Britain, which was at
first refused.

In August 1775 Colonel William Faucitt was sent to Germany to
muster the Hanoverian battalions, after which he was sent to see
what he could accomplish at the courts of Brunswick and Hesse–
Cassel. By the arrangements made with these and other German
states Britain obtained the services of some 30,000 mercenaries.[1]
The storm of indignation which this aroused was unjustified as there
were several precedents. German troops had been brought to
England during both the 1715 and 1745 highland rebellions. More
recently, the Royal American Regiment, composed largely of
foreigners, had been used, without any objections from the colonies
involved, to keep order among the turbulent frontiersmen of
Virginia and Pennsylvania.

The first of several treaties was signed with Duke Charles I of
Brunswick on 9 January 1776. By its terms he agreed to provide a
corps of 4,300 well-equipped officers and men. This consisted of a
small general staff, a regiment of dismounted dragoons (whom the
British government agreed to provide with horses should the need
arise), four regiments of infantry, a battalion of grenadiers and
another of light infantry. He was to keep them in uniforms, accoutre-

---

[1] Strictly speaking these troops were not mercenaries, who sold their services
individually, but regular troops hired as a body, nevertheless they are generally
referred to as such.

ments, and arms, in return for which he was to receive a bounty of roughly £7 sterling per recruit, and a subsidy of nearly £12,000 per year until their return to Brunswick, and twice that amount per annum for two years thereafter. In addition he was to be paid a sum equal to the levy for each soldier killed, incapacitated, or taken prisoner, and the same amount for every three men wounded. The officers and men were to receive pay and allowances on the same scale as the British army. The Duke sent altogether 5,723 officers and men to America, of whom only 2,708 returned to their homeland.

On 22 February the troops left Wolfenbüttel for their port of embarkation, Stade on the Elbe, where the dragoons and grenadier battalion embarked on 5 March. The force sailed in two divisions, the first commanded by Major-General v. Riedesel consisting of the Dragoon Regiment Prinz Ludwig, the Grenadier Battalion composed of the grenadier companies of the four infantry regiments, and the regiments Prinz Friedrich and v. Riedesel. The second division commanded by Colonel v. Specht consisted of the Light Infantry Battalion, which included a company of jägers, and the regiments v. Specht and v. Rhetz. Both divisions were sent to Quebec and took part in Burgoyne's ill-fated expedition. The surrender of his force at Saratoga on 16 October 1777 saw the end of the Brunswick corps as a fighting unit.

The second treaty was signed on 15 January 1776 with the Landgrave Federick II of Hesse-Cassel, perhaps the wealthiest of all the other German principalities. He could bring 40,000 troops into the field, 'as good as any in all Germany' as Colonel Hanger, who served with them, put it. This was the sixth time in 100 years that Hessian troops had been hired out to Great Britain. They had served on the Continent in 1739, 1740, and 1742, and together with Dutch troops on British soil in 1746. The Landgrave agreed to provide a corps of 12,000 men consisting of four grenadier battalions, fifteen infantry regiments, two companies of jägers, and sufficient artillerymen to man the two pieces attached to each infantry regiment. The jägers were a mounted unit, but like the Brunswick Dragoons, they brought no horses or saddlery with them.

Being already wealthy and able to prolong the negotiations in his interest, Frederick II got the best of the bargain with the British, for while his treaty was essentially the same as that with Brunswick the bounty was more than twice as high. He was to receive almost

£110,000 a year until one year after his corps returned to Cassel. There was, however, no blood-money clause, although his own Paymaster-General in America could pocket the pay of deceased soldiers for a time as payment was made for the number of men at the last annual muster. In addition he managed to get paid a long-standing and disputed claim for £42,000 for hospital services during the Seven Years War.

The Hessian troops were superior to those sent by the other German princes. Their discipline and training was the same as that of the Prussians, but, according to Colonel Hanger, 'In one respect the preference may be given to them, the Hessian regiments being composed all of *landes kinder* (natives of the country), whereas the Prussians have a great number of foreigners in their battalions'. Nevertheless the Landgrave had to do some rapid recruiting to meet his treaty obligations, and each of the fifteen infantry regiments was brought up to the full strength of a grenadier company and five battalion companies. The grenadier companies, together with the Grenadier Regiment v. Rall, and two companies from the Regiment Garde, provided the four grenadier battalions of four companies each.

Like the Brunswick troops, the Hessians left Bremen in two divisions, the first consisting of the regiments Leib, Erbprinz, Prinz Carl, v. Ditfurth, v. Lossberg, v. Knyphausen, v. Trümbach, v. Mirbach, v. Rall, and part of the artillery. They sailed on 17 April and arrived at Staten Island on 15 August in time to take part in the Battle of Long Island. The second division, which arrived in New York in October, consisted of the regiments v. Wutginau, v. Wissembach, v. Bunau, v. Stein, v. Huyn, the jägers, and the remainder of the artillery.

Hesse-Cassel sent 17,000 officers and men to North America out of a population of less than 300,000 and of these less than two-thirds returned home. The greater proportion of those who failed to return, however, remained in America as settlers.

On 5 February 1776, a treaty was signed with Duke William of Hesse-Hanau, the son of Frederick II of Hesse-Cassel, for one infantry regiment and one artillery company totalling 900 men. The blood money clause was included and as with the other treaties the services of the troops were confined to North America. The Duke benefited to the tune of £10,000 per year. Some 2,400 troops, including 400 recruits sent out in 1781 and 1782, served in America, mostly in Canada, of whom only 1,400 returned home. Duke William and his father were the only rulers to reduce the taxes of families who had a member serving in British pay.

On 17 March a treaty was signed with Prince Frederick of Waldeck, whose country had long been a source of mercenaries, recruited by compulsory military service to which all his subjects except students were liable. In spite of the fact that he already had eight infantry battalions in Dutch service the Prince agreed to provide a fully equipped corps consisting of a regiment of infantry and a small train of artillery to be ready by 6 May. The bounty was to be 30 crowns per recruit, the annual subsidy 20,050 crowns, and the blood money clause was included. By ruthless conscription and by recalling troops from Holland, the Prince managed to raise some 1,225 men who arrived at New Rochelle with the second Hesse-Cassel Division in October 1776. They served for several years in the Floridas and less than half ever saw their fatherland again.

The fifth treaty was signed on 1 February 1777 with the Margrave Charles Alexander of Anspach-Bayreuth for two Brandenburg-Anspach infantry regiments of 570 men each, an Anspach-Bayreuth jäger company of 101 men, and an artillery company of forty-four men, totalling 1,285 officers and men. The treaty, which did not contain the blood money clause, brought to the Margrave's depleted treasury no less than a quarter of a million pounds. The plan was to ship the men from Ochsenfurth-on-Main to the Dutch coast, where they were embarked on 9 March. Their quarters, however, were so bad that they mutinied the next day, and the following day the Margrave personally intervened to restore order. They arrived at New York on 3 June 1777. The passage of a later contingent through Brandenburg was refused by Frederick the Great. Anspach-Bayreuth sent some 2,353 officers and men to America of whom almost half failed to return.

In October 1777 the sixth and last treaty was signed with the absentee Prince Frederick Augustus of Anhalt-Zerbst, brother of Catherine the Great, whose small state with its population of 20,000 was probably the poorest country within the German Empire. In spite of great difficulties in finding and transporting recruits to the port of Stade, the Prince managed to send one infantry regiment of two battalions totalling 1,119 men to America. With extra recruits sent in April 1781 a total of 1,152 served at Quebec and all but 168 returned home.

In 1776, the first full year of war, some 20,000 German auxiliary troops arrived to help the British in North America. The strength of this force, which almost equalled that of the regular British army, remained constant throughout the war. Further treaties were made, from time to time, for additional companies of jägers who were found to be particularly useful in America.

The two largest contingents from Hesse-Cassel and Brunswick were similar in appearance if not in quality. The rank and file of the Hesse-Cassel units, which made up the larger part of the German troops sent to America, were largely regulars, many of whom had seen service during the Seven Years War, although in the later years of the war conscription and the press-gang became necessary. The officers were career soldiers, most of whom had seen active service. Many were members of the lesser nobility and seem to have received a fairly good education, although their lack of English was to prove an embarrassment in America.

The Hesse-Cassel troops were the only ones who were to be employed as a unit under their own general officers, and according to the treaty arrangements were only to be separated when necessary. Each of the infantry regiments consisted of two battalions, one of fusiliers and one of musketeers (although this was only a nominal distinction), with some 120 grenadiers distributed among the two battalions. Following the British custom of the time the grenadiers were concentrated into battalions.

The place of the regimental light infantry was taken by the companies of jägers, sometimes called *chasseurs*, both words meaning 'hunter'. They were light troops, both horse and foot, recruited from huntsmen, gamekeepers and foresters, and they were armed with rifles. Since they were found to be especially effective against the American riflemen, a request for more jägers was sent to London immediately after the battle of Long Island. In a separate treaty of December 1776 the quota of jägers was raised by the Landgrave Hesse-Cassel from 260 to 1,067, provided, however, that 'experienced chasseurs, all well-trained marksmen' could be obtained. It is doubtful if the total number of effective jägers in America ever succeeded 700, and not all these were Hessians.

The jäger corps, which was organised in the summer of 1777

under the command of Colonel v. Wurmb, included both Hesse-Hanau and Anspach jägers. They were employed in detached parties for reconnaissance and patrol duties, and for guarding foraging parties and headquarters. During several campaigns jäger detachments were attached to infantry regiments and were used either leading the van, or flanking the column, on the march, or forming the flanks when the troops formed in line. When in retreat they formed the rearguard. The jägers, who carried no bayonets, were not very good at protecting themselves. On one occasion, Clinton asked the commander of the Hessians to provide George Hanger (a captain in the Hessian jäger corps), with two hundred volunteers from the line battalions. So his small command was strengthened by a 'body of men with bayonets, who might by night be employed to greater effect than the Jaegers, who had no bayonets, and were armed only with rifle-guns'.

The Hesse-Cassel infantry was organised into four brigades of line infantry and one of grenadiers, and the corps had its own general staff, hospital and supply train. Each regiment of infantry and each company of jägers had two small field-pieces as supporting weapons.

The regiments and battalions were named after their *chefs*, either one of the princes or the commanding officer, with the exception of one unit, the *Leib* (Guard) Regiment. When a colonel was transferred or died, the name of his command was changed to that of the new *chef*. During periods when the command was vacant regiments were known as '*alt* (or formerly) so-and-so'.

The uniforms of the Hesse-Cassel infantry were virtually indistinguishable from those of the Prussian army and were similarly made of coarse and cheap material. They were too hot for summer and too cold for winter, nor had the men any greatcoats apart from the watchcoats kept specifically for sentries. The infantry wore medium blue coats with lapels and cuffs of regimental colours, white, yellow or 'straw' waistcoats and breeches, and black gaiters. The musketeers wore tricorne cocked hats garnished with worsted pompoms and tassels, while the fusiliers and grenadiers wore special mitre caps, with metal fronts emblazoned with various heraldic devices.

The officers had ornamental embroidered button-holes on their coats, gorgets, and silver net waist-sashes with large tassels, but gradually the embroideries were removed and the officers were ordered to dress their hair like their men and to carry fusils instead of espontoons.

The Hessian officers at the beginning of the New York campaign went on foot, with their cloaks rolled round their shoulders, and a large gourd-shaped flask of rum and water at their side. Many of them slung their fusils on the march and even Colonel v. Donop could be seen taking part in the firing during an action. After the first engagements the troops were permitted to wear their sword waist-belts over their shoulders.

The equipment of the men consisted of a large fur knapsack slung over one shoulder, and a large tin water-canteen on a buff leather strap. Over the other shoulder went a broad buff belt which supported the black leather cartouche box which was decorated with a brass or white metal plate.

The jägers wore green with crimson facings and the artillery blue with crimson facings.

The Brunswick troops were dressed in a similar manner but had 'old and bad clothing'. The cut was tight and skimpy, while the facings, collars and cuffs were mere strips of coloured cloth sewn on to the coats, with cheap and plain buttons. In fact they were so bad that the British government had to advance General v. Riedesel £5,000 to dress his men properly. An inspecting officer at Stade noted that the Brunswickers were 'far from making a fine body of men, having a greater number of small and ill-looking and many old people among them'. The second division of Hessians which arrived at New York in October 1776 was also 'unpromising in appearance' but fought well at Fort Washington. They were largely recruits and drafts from the militia and the garrison regiments.

General Haldimond who commanded in Canada spoke of the Hesse-Hanau drafts which arrived in September 1778 as 'the refuse of those who accompanied Burgoyne', with few exceptions 'both by nature and education unfit for an American war'. Haldimond also spoke of some recently arrived German recruits as 'picked up on the highways . . . rather a burthen than an increase of strength'.

The behaviour of the Brunswick troops that fought with Burgoyne has been criticised, but there is no question about their courage and soldierly qualities. Burgoyne admitted that the expedition required the utmost speed and enthusiasm, and hinted that the German troops were not exactly afire for the cause. The Germans brought with them neither a loyalty for England nor a dislike of

America, and the exclusion of their commander General v. Riedesel from Burgoyne's council of war may have had a dampening effect upon their ardour. It was noted that the German battalions moved in a leisurely and spiritless way, encumbered by their haversacks, long-skirted coats, long swords, enormous canteens, grenadier caps with heavy brass ornaments, much powder and pomatum in the hair, and clumsy queues. So laden they jogged their way gloomily through dense forests and over impassable roads, sick of mercenary warfare and longing for their dear fatherland.

As for the Hessians, neither officers nor men knew much about the causes of the war, and to them the Americans were rebels who refused to obey their lawful king. Having sworn allegiance to this same king they were bound to fight these rebels for him. Their innate discipline made them good soldiers and as such they fought for a cause in which they had no concern.

The Hesse-Cassel troops took part in every major engagement of the war after their arrival in America. For instance ten regiments took part in the attack on Fort Washington which surrendered to the German commander v. Knyphausen and was renamed in his honour; nine took part in the battles of Long Island and Brandy-wine; seven were at White Plains; six at Newport and Charleston, and five at Springfield. Jäger detachments participated in all the engagements except some minor skirmishes in the south.

The Hessians were certainly not the ogres they have been painted to be. At first they were feared by the civil population, but as the war progressed they were generally better liked and more civilly treated than the British. When prisoners-of-war the Hessian officers and even the common soldiers were frequently shown favours never bestowed on their British comrades, mainly in order to persuade them to desert after being exchanged.

The German officers returned home after the war with valuable experience acquired in America. In the wars that followed, the German leaders who had trained in the school of Frederick the Great were too old for active service, and their place was taken by many who had served in America. The Hessian jäger officer Johann Ewald eventually became a general in the Danish service and the author of several influential works on guerrilla warfare and light troops. The writings of General v. Ochs were adopted by Frederick the Great who, in his last years, raised three light infantry regiments, trained by a number of officers who had served in America. The celebrated v. Gneisenau, who also served as a jäger, raised nineteen battalions of light troops trained on the American model. Indeed one contemporary, a Prussian general, has asserted that of all France's adversaries during the revolutionary campaigns of 1792–1794, the troops of Hesse-Cassel were the best disciplined.

3

LOYALISTS

One of the aspects of the American revolution most mismanaged by
the British government was its treatment of those colonists who
remained loyal to the Crown, the 'Loyalists', or, as the rebels[1]
preferred to call them, the 'Tories'. Throughout the first three years
of the war the British believed that the loyalists were in the majority,
and that the revolution was merely the work of a dissident minority.
But in spite of this belief Britain failed to develop a consistent,
vigorous, policy that would have made full use of loyalist support.

At the appearance of open resistance Loyalist Associations were
formed in nearly every colony, encouraged by General Gage at
Boston and by several of the royal governors. As a result the British
government was inundated with requests to raise Provincial corps,
and for temporary military support until such corps could be
organised, but through ill-preparedness more than a year elapsed
before any significant action was taken in the matter. During the first
year of active warfare, however, loyalists were used extensively,
their importance temporarily inflated by the shortage of British
troops, the lack of vigorous leadership, 3,000 miles of sea, and the
activity of the rebels. In these unfavourable circumstances the
loyalists seemed to offer a last chance to nip the rebellion in the
bud.

The first corps of loyalists, 300 strong, was raised in Massachusetts
in the autumn of 1774 by Colonel Thomas Gilbert, but in April of
the following year he was forced to flee to Boston and his corps was
broken up. After Lexington and Concord, loyalist refugees flocked
to Boston where Gage approved the formation of at least three small
units, but even the most promising of these, the Loyal American
Associators, formed by Timothy Ruggles, was of disappointing
quality. Nova Scotia, however, more loyal than Massachusetts, was
the scene of more effective attempts. As early as April 1775, colonels
Allan Maclean and Joseph Gorham had their proposals to raise
corps of 'His Majesty's Loyal North American Subjects' approved.
Maclean, planning to recruit recent emigrants from the Scottish

---

[1] The term 'rebel' has been used from time to time, instead of the more compli-
mentary 'revolutionary' or 'patriot', because that is the way in which the enemy
was usually referred to in British despatches and letters of the time.

highlands, sent recruiting officers into North Carolina, New York, Nova Scotia and Canada. Maclean's corps became the Royal Highland Emigrants, Gorham's the Royal Fencible Americans, and a third corps, raised in Nova Scotia by Governor Francis Legge, the Loyal Nova Scotia Volunteers. While not as successful as their promoters predicted, these undertakings made a vital contribution to the defence of Canada and Nova Scotia, at a time when the rebel capture of Crown Point and Ticonderoga threatened the northern provinces.

In September 1775, the British governor of Fort Pitt, John Connolly, proposed the setting up of an army 'to the Westward for alarming the frontiers of Virginia, Maryland, Pennsylvania, and New York', and was authorised to raise a battalion of loyalists, the Loyal Foresters. At the same time Alexander McKee, Deputy Superintendent of Indian Affairs at Fort Pitt, was to raise a body of Indian auxiliaries. These two units, with some British regulars, were to march from Fort Pitt in the spring of 1776 to Alexandria, Virginia, where the loyalist Governor Dunmore intended to take the offensive. This promising plan was cut short when McKee was captured by the rebels in November 1775.

In the winter and spring of 1776 an abortive expedition to South Carolina ended with the humiliating British attempt to capture Fort Moultrie in Charleston harbour. The main object of the expedition had been to bring aid to the numerous loyalists whom, it was reported, were determined to throw off the rebel yoke in the southern states. In spite of the failure of the expedition, however, the response of the loyalists was such that a belief in the loyalty of the southern states persisted, until schemes to make use of them eventually dominated British strategy.

By the middle of 1776 the situation had changed considerably, with Britain now ready to launch a major offensive with a large army of regular troops. The loyalists were, for the moment, pushed into the background since well-trained professionals rather than lightly regarded Provincials were needed to make a show of force. The ensuing Long Island campaign was successful, and by the autumn Howe was in control of New York and most of New Jersey. British prestige among the loyalists was high, but before full advantage could be taken of the situation, Washington struck at Trenton, and the opportunity passed. The ebb of British fortunes sowed doubts among the more timid loyalists, while others reacted angrily to the excesses committed by the British while in pursuit of Washington through New Jersey. The rejection of Governor Tryon's plan to make New York a loyalist stronghold, and the offer of pardons to all those rebels who would take the oath of allegiance to the Crown, alienated the loyalists even more.

Nevertheless several Provincial regiments were raised at this time. Apart from the three Provincial units based in Nova Scotia, Turnbull's New York Volunteers raised in January 1776, and the King's Royal Regiment of New York formed by Sir John Johnson in June 1776, most of the important permanent Provincial corps were raised after the capture of New York in September 1776. During the summer Oliver Delancey raised three battalions of the New York Loyalists, Cortlandt Skinner six battalions of the New Jersey Loyalists, and the celebrated Robert Rogers, the Queen's Rangers. These regiments became the strongest of all the Provincial corps and later were among the most reliable. During the winter of 1776–1777 Edmund Fanning raised the King's American Regiment, Beverley Robinson the Loyal American Regiment, and Montforte Browne the Prince of Wales's American Regiment. Later in 1777 a corps of Pennsylvania loyalists was raised by William Allen, and another, of Maryland loyalists, by John Chalmers. At the same time Howe appointed a Paymaster-General, a Muster-Master General, and an Inspector General of Provincials. These units, chiefly recruited from the loyalists of the middle provinces, formed the nucleus of the 'Provincial Service', for although less than a third of the number of corps raised during the war, they contained nearly two-thirds of all those loyalists who took up arms.

When, in 1777, Britain altered her policy and decided to make greater use of potential loyalists, she found that they did not respond as anticipated. After being ignored and even plundered during the New York campaign, they did not eagerly flock to join the British army when given the opportunity, and recruiting figures were disappointing. As early as August 1776 clothing and equipment for 7,000 Provincials were prepared for shipment from Britain, and after Howe's victory at Long Island a further 3,000 sets were assembled. Months later, however, there were slightly more than 3,000 loyalists under arms, and although the Provincial line grew to approximately 8,000 in the following three years, the British authorities were greatly disappointed. The loss of 5,000 troops at Saratoga in October 1777 and the entry of France into the war combined to force a reappraisal of British military policy. This, coupled with the disappointing recruiting figures, led in 1778 to a re-examination of the existing Provincial regulations. Each recruit was now to receive, in lieu of levy money, a royal grant of fifty acres; recruits were to serve for two years or 'during the present war in North America'; and all Provincials, while on active service, were to receive the same pay as regulars. However Provincial officers serving with regulars were ranked below them, nor were they entitled to permanent rank or half-pay on reduction.

The reforms, proposed by a board of general officers, and made effective in December 1778, included a bounty of three guineas for each new Provincial recruit, an allowance of one guinea for the apprehension of each Provincial deserter, and an annual allowance of £40 to each Provincial regiment for hospital expenses, nurses and orderly rooms. These were followed, in May 1779, by the granting of permanent rank in America, and half-pay for Provincial officers of corps completed to the same establishment as regular regiments, which were also 'properly officered and fit for service'. Provincial officers who lost a limb, or were maimed, were to receive the same gratuity of one year's pay in advance as regular officers. Further steps taken to improve recruiting were an additional bounty of 22/6d, encouragement to recruits from the Continental army, and the assurance given to fugitives from justice that every effort would be made to secure their pardon.

The results, however, remained disappointing, for while in 1779, the total strength of the Provincial corps had increased less than 20 per cent, in 1780 and 1781, there were scarcely enough recruits to replace casualties and desertions. When several Provincial corps were placed on the Regular Establishment many Provincial officers redoubled their recruiting efforts in order to qualify for permanent rank and half-pay, but the anticipated expansion of the Provincial service never materialised. In May 1779 a new 'American Establishment' was created and the Queen's Rangers became the 1st American Regiment, the Volunteers of Ireland became the 2nd, the New York Volunteers became the 3rd, the King's American Regiment the 4th, and the British Legion the 5th.

From the outset, the British government assumed that large numbers of loyalists could be employed by forming them into Provincial regiments for service alongside the regulars. In the past, however, no satisfactory working arrangement had been developed between the

Provincials and the regulars, and the various attempts to find one had tended to create mutual distrust between the two. For their part the British army had found Provincials inefficient, poorly disciplined, and composed of sickly, ignorant riffraff. The Provincials, equally aggrieved, found the British arrogant, overbearing and condescending. In addition to the disadvantages already mentioned the Provincial officer found himself assigned to a lower social position.

After 1775 the British government considered raising Provincial regiments 'for rank'. By this system prominent loyalists were given the command of corps, with the right to nominate some officers, on condition that a stipulated number of recruits were raised within a specified period. The advantage of this system to the government was that the colonels bore many of the recruiting expenses, only drew pay when their corps were three-quarters complete and were ineligible for half-pay. While it was known that loyalists were averse to enlisting in regular regiments, every report indicated that numerous 'friends of government' would readily join loyalist corps raised 'for rank'. The objections to this system, apart from the fact that the King disliked both Provincial corps and regiments raised for rank, were that the loyalists on the whole lacked military experience, required months of training and were not available for immediate service. Moreover Provincial officers were generally appointed for their ability to find recruits, rather than for any demonstrated leadership and military knowledge. Another problem was that Britain was generally unable to find the necessary rank and file to fill up Provincial regiments, yet could not employ the many loyalists who were 'of a rank in life superior to the class from which the common seaman and soldier are taken'.

The majority of the Provincial corps consisted of line infantry, with the usual grenadier and light infantry companies, but there was also a sprinkling of light infantry, rangers, and light dragoons, who in some cases were formed into legions of horse and foot. At first there were no uniforms; the earliest Boston units, for example, were distinguished by different field-signs such as cockades and armbands. After the capture of New York, bulk clothing was sent out from England for the use of the Provincials. By the spring of 1778 some 10,000 suits of green regimentals, with white buttons, and white, blue or red facings had been supplied. With them came white waistcoats and breeches, dark brown gaiters, hats and accoutrements of standard British design. The weapons were the same as those issued to the regulars, although in many cases the Provincials received the older 'Long Land' model of Brown Bess.

In 1778 it was decided to clothe the Provincials in red, and further supplies were sent out, with white, buff, orange, blue, green or black facings. Waistcoats and breeches were white except for those regiments with buff facings. Henceforth the custom seems to have been adopted of buying up clothing left in store by regiments ordered home, and uniforms of the 10th, 46th, and 52nd regiments all passed into Provincial service. While the majority of colonels seemed happy at the change to red coats, some like Colonel Simcoe of the Queen's Rangers fought hard to keep their green clothing. The light dragoons were at first dressed in red, but later the Philadelphia light Dragoons, the Bucks County Dragoons and James's Troop of Provincial Dragoons – all raised in Philadelphia – were ordered into green so that they could serve with the Queen's Rangers.

After 1778 the British, encouraged by continuing forecasts of a vigorous loyalist response, confined their major offensives to the southern colonies. As an experiment to test both the response of the southern loyalists, and Washington's reaction to an attack on the southern colonies, an expedition was first sent to Georgia. After the rapid capture of Savannah in January 1779 the British commanders, Campbell and Prevost, unwisely extended their control into areas which could only be held with the strong support of the loyalists. This was a pattern which was to be repeated in the southern colonies for the remainder of the war. With no plan to follow up their initial success, they carried out a series of operations which aroused opposition without either destroying the enemy or restoring peace to the conquered territory. After eight months of periodic attacks on the rebels, and frequent appeals to the loyalists, the British held little beyond the environs of Savannah.

Although Clinton had begun to plan further operations in the south in March 1779, the late-arrival of expected reinforcements, the preparations for an expedition to Jamaica and the French siege of Savannah delayed the southern campaign for the rest of the year. Learning that the siege had been lifted, Clinton sailed for Charleston with nearly 8,000 rank and file on 26 December. The subsequent siege and capture of Charleston shattered American resistance in the accepted terms. The need was now for wise measures to pacify the country, but as before in Georgia, they were not forthcoming. In

July 1780 Clinton returned to New York leaving Cornwallis in charge of the subjugation of South Carolina.

The British plan was that once this had been done Cornwallis would extend his operations northward into North Carolina, and thence into the Chesapeake and the middle colonies. This plan was dependent on the formation of a loyal militia in South Carolina. For a time Major Patrick Ferguson, who was appointed Inspector of Militia and Major Commandant of the first battalion, made considerable progress among the loyalists of the Ninety-Six district, raising eight battalions by the middle of July, from which some 1,500 men could be drawn to operate with the army. But elsewhere results were mixed. In strongly loyalist areas an effective militia was raised which maintained local control until Cornwallis abandoned the Carolinas in April 1781. In Charleston itself 400 loyalists carried out patrol and guard duties, so releasing further troops for service in the field. But in other districts, notably Camden, Cheraw and Georgetown, all strong rebel centres, the militia was unreliable and in July one entire battalion went over to the enemy. In addition attempts to raise two South Carolina Provincial battalions were conspicuous failures, largely through a shortage of good officer material, as were efforts to fill the ranks of established Provincial units by recruiting in the south.

In October Cornwallis started his march northwards to rally the North Carolina loyalists, and to cut off support for the South Carolina rebels, while Ferguson marched on a parallel course through the back-country. On the 7th, Ferguson was defeated and killed at King's Mountain, and Cornwallis was forced to halt. Before he could resume the campaign the situation in the south had changed completely. The destruction of Ferguson's loyalists at King's Mountain and the arrival of another American army under General Greene put an end to any prospect of organising the Carolina loyalists. Cornwallis therefore prepared for another campaign in North Carolina in conjunction with the force commanded by Leslie, which had recently arrived in the Chesapeake, with the object of clearing the southern colonies of armed rebels. When disaster struck a second time at Cowpens on 17 January 1781, he struck back blindly at Morgan and Greene, losing both his baggage and the crucial race to the Dan River. In February Cornwallis found himself several hundred miles away from his nearest support, totally inequipped to complete his original plans for the North Carolina loyalists.

Gradually he abandoned the loyalist experiment, which was the prime purpose of the southern campaign. After a bloody engagement with Greene at Guildford Courthouse, he made another appeal to the loyalists to rally to the royal standard, but encountered a very meagre response. So he abandoned the Carolinas to the rebels, convinced that any campaign dependant upon co-operation from the loyalists was doomed to failure.

Peace in the south depended upon reconciling the rebels to British authority and upon rapidly organising the loyalists to quell any minor rebel resurgence. When the excesses of the army, ill-advised regulations governing former rebels, rumours of approaching aid from the north, and the natural difficulties of subduing a vast frontier region finally precipitated a 'second revolution' in the south, the small army of Cornwallis proved unequal to the challenge. Britain overestimated the strength of her friends in America, failing to distinguish between mere friendship and a willingness to take an active part in the war. The loyalist virtues – conservatism, caution, and peaceableness – were military weaknesses, and the reputation of the British army was itself encouragement enough for the loyalists to stand aside while the regulars crushed the rebellion.

Britain's basic strategy after Saratoga rested squarely upon the participation of the loyalists in the re-establishment of royal authority in America, and not until Cornwallis abandoned the Carolinas and marched into Virginia, and ultimately to Yorktown, did a high-ranking officer repudiate these plans. Clinton expressed doubts, but continued his efforts to make the loyalist experiment succeed, until his efforts were frustrated by the breakdown in communications between himself and Cornwallis during the summer of 1781. Although military operations virtually ceased after Yorktown, the Provincials remained serving until the end of the war, when some 40,000 loyalists fled to Canada.

Britain made two fatal errors in dealing with the loyalists. First, she turned to them for assistance much too late, and then she placed too complete a reliance on them.

4

INDIANS

Apart from their German mercenaries and the loyalists, the British had the dubious assistance of the 770 tomahawks and scalping-knives which it was estimated that the British Indians could bring into the field against the colonists. These Indians were employed against the frontiers of New York, Pennsylvania and Virginia. Chief among them were the Iroquois, the celebrated confederacy of the Six Nations, who dwelt in the fertile lands between Lake Ontario in the west and the Mohawk River in the east.

The most westerly and largest of the five original tribes, the Seneca, occupied the country around the Genesee River; next to them to the east their nearest eastern neighbours were the Cayugas; then came the Onondagas, the Oneidas along the shores of the lake of that name, and lastly the dreaded Mohawks. The Tuscaroras, who were taken into the confederation in the early years of the century, lived to the south-east along the banks of the east branch of the Susquehanna.

The Iroquois had created an advanced political and social system, the leaders of which met at least every five years in federal council. In and around their well-built villages they raised horses, cattle, pigs and chickens, tended extensive orchards and grew a variety of vegetables. Their staple food was corn eaten either on the cob, or pounded into meal to make bread. They hunted but although fish were plentiful they were difficult to catch and large game, such as deer or bear, was scarce. But for all their plenty the Iroquois were improvident and either unwilling, or unable, to store provisions for the long winters and springs.

In appearance the Iroquois were generally tall and athletic, being trained from early childhood to endure extremes of pain and inclement weather. They had high angular cheek bones, brown eyes, high-bridged aquiline noses, full lips, and straight black hair. In colour they varied from a warm ruddy-tan brown to a light olive. The beard and eyebrows were very sparse, and any stray hairs were plucked out. Most warriors shaved their heads, cutting the hair, or plucking it out, or even rubbing it off with hot stones, as close to the head as possible, except for a tuft the size of the palm of the hand, which was left to grow about two inches long on the crown. In the centre of this tuft was a scalp lock which was allowed to grow and was braided and passed through a small carved bone ornament. This lock was scrupulously preserved so that a victorious enemy could take it in battle and also served as an attachment for the roach, or crest, made of deer's tail and moose hair surmounted or decorated with turkey's feathers and porcupine's quills, which was fastened to it by a piece of bone. The roach and the greater part of the head were dyed vermilion.

Great pains were taken over the application of the ceremonial 'warpaint'. Vermilion was the most popular colour, followed by charcoal, ochre and vegetable green. Many tribes tattooed themselves with a mixture of charcoal and vermilion.

The Iroquois were a military force to be reckoned with, specialising in guerrilla warfare of extreme ferocity and absolute ruthlessness. They were taught the arts of war from an early age in training exercises held outside the villages, when groups of children, armed with wooden knives and with plaited scalp locks of wheat, fought fiercely in mock battles. The Iroquois braves were expert scouts and could move through thick forest, the exposed tops of the taller wind-blown trees providing some guide to their direction. With their highly developed sense of smell they could detect the smoke of enemy fires at great distances, and could read the tracks on a woodland path with an expertness the white frontiersman could not approach. The Iroquois were early exponents of the art of 'fire and movement' as the following contemporary description of their tactics shows. When they had advanced close enough to use their rifles, we are told,

> they proceed by divisions, so as always to keep up a constant fire – while one division advances and fires while the next is holding on and so on – In general except upon very important cases they carryh (*sic*) on a kind of desaltory warfare which must be very distressing to an enemy; they go out in small parties, conceil themselves under the bushes and when they see an opportunity of gaining any advantage, they Sally forth and are guided according to circumstances.

More than a hundred years earlier the Frenchman Champlain and his Huron allies had massacred the Iroquois at Ticonderoga and ever since their victims had allied themselves with the enemies of

France, first the Dutch, and then the British. In the so-called 'King George's War', and the French-Indian war, Sir William Johnson, His Majesy's Superintendent of Indian Affairs (a Mohawk chief and the second Baronet to be created in America), had managed to keep the frontier between the French and English intact with the help of the Iroquois.

At Albany in 1746 he had succeeded in welding the Six Nations into a fighting force ready to take the warpath to Canada. By the time the war had ended in 1748, Johnson, in command of the whole northern department of New York State's military establishment, was the most important man in the Mohawk valley. After the 1754 Albany Conference, called by New York, Massachusetts, New Hampshire, Connecticut, Rhode Island, Pennsylvania and Maryland, Johnson was made Superintendent in an attempt to regulate Indian affairs.

In 1761, during the Seven Years War, a grand council of the nations was held at Detroit, with 500 sachems and warriors representing seven western tribes as well as the Six Nations, in the hope that the status and allegiance of the Indians would be settled once and for all. Two years later the indifference and parsimony of the British Commander-in-Chief Amherst led to the rising of Pontiac, Chief of the Ottawas, which loosed the full terror of Indian war on the frontier. Even the Six Nations were affected, for the most westerly tribe, the Senecas, who had always been the least trustworthy and most susceptible to French influence, joined Pontiac's war parties. The borders of Pennsylvania and Virginia bore the brunt of the terror and every fort in the west except Detroit was lost by Indian treachery. Amherst was recalled and Gage appointed to his place. At length, in July 1764, largely through the efforts of Sir William Johnson, a great peace council was held at Niagara attended by 1,400 tribesmen.

With the fall of France, however, the Indians lost their bargaining power. Before, when their painted warriors had tipped the balance between rival military establishments, they had been courted and cajoled. Now they were to be pushed rudely aside. Supervision of the Indian trade was passed over to the Provincial governments who allowed all controls to lapse in favour of the frontiersmen. In 1768 Johnson called a conference of the Indians at Fort Stanwix on the upper Mohawk, and at the cost of large concessions of land, a permanent boundary line was fixed between the hunting grounds of the Indians and the white men. The 'Stanwix Line' was, however, soon violated by trappers, traders and speculators. In attempting to protect its Indian allies the British government alienated large groups of stubborn and determined frontiersmen, who soon sided with the discontented merchants and shippers in denouncing the Crown's interference with what they maintained were their 'natural rights'.

When Silver Heels, the old Senaca scout, who had served General Braddock and other Englishmen all his life, was brutally murdered and scalped by white men, 600 tribesmen gathered at Johnson Hall demanding justice. Unhappily, soon after addressing them on July 11, Sir William Johnson died, and was succeeded in the baronetcy by his son John.

It had taken Great Britain fifteen years to win over the affections of the tribes from the French and to attach them to the British Crown; with the outbreak of the revolution the rebels sought to break down this relationship. Before attacking Ticonderoga in May 1775, Ethan Allen appealed to them to ambush the regulars in exchange for money, blankets, tomahawks and knives. The loyalty of the Indians was such that his message was swiftly passed on to the British authorities in Canada. But not all the Indians were loyal, for the Mohicans of Stockbridge and the Oneidas, one of the Six Nations, ranged themselves on the side of the colonists, and performed good service as scouts throughout the contest. In June Colonel Guy Carleton organised a conference of the Six Nations at Montreal, where each of the assembled tribes was given a war belt, war songs were sung, and Sir John Johnson urged them to rise up and attack the rebels. When they agreed, however, Carleton rejected their offer to lay waste the New England frontier on humanitarian grounds, and much to their disgust accepted only the help of a party of some fifty braves to act as scouts. A few months later the American General Schuyler at another conference, tried with some success to persuade the Indians to remain neutral. In 1776 Sir John Johnson was driven out of Johnson Hall and fled with the Indians, first to Fort Stanwix, then to Oswego and finally to Fort Niagara, which became the active headquarters of the Indian Superintendence and the rendezvous for their raiding parties.

A renewed offer of help was accepted by Carleton, and in the following year when Burgoyne's expedition set out he was accompanied by parties of Iroquois and the now reconciled Algonquins.

This use of 'savages' was bitterly criticised by Whigs in London, although they had been used in previous wars in North America, but Burgoyne regarded them as essential for forest operations. They were not, however, all from the Six Nations, as the following list reveals. It was included in a letter from General Phillips to Simon Fraser dated 10 September 1776.

Carleton	Nipisains	90	*Fraser*	Six Nations	56
	Algonquins	90		Outawaughs	24
	Of the Lakes	80		Abanakis	79
	Coinewaughs	121			
	St Regis	110			

Joseph Brant, along with 1,000 warriors of the Senecas, Tuscaroras, Mississagies and Mohawks, was to accompany Barry St Leger on his diversionary sweep down the Mohawk.

When Burgoyne was at Fort Anne in July, Jane McCrea, the fiancée of a loyalist officer, was tomahawked to death by one of a pair of Indians escorting her to the British camp from rebel-held territory, and the story was immediately used by the rebels to inflame the New England townships. Burgoyne's crude and arrogant handling of the Indians did not calm their seething discontent. After the disastrous expedition to Bennington, when many Indians died including the 'Grand Chief', the remainder deserted Burgoyne.

In the period of deadlock which followed immediately after the American success at Saratoga, Sir John Johnson, now Colonel of the loyalist King's Royal Regiment, better known as 'Johnson's Greens', rallied the Iroquois, swept down the Mohawk valley and raided the isolated frontier hamlets, pillaging, burning and scalping. In this he was assisted by Major John Butler, his son Walter and his celebrated Rangers.

In 1778 Colonel van Schaik with 558 men descended on the homelands of the Onondagas, killing thirty-three warriors and burning crops and buildings. The Onondagas were determined to retaliate and 300 of them, led by Brant, attacked Schoharie. At the 'Battle of Minnisink' sixty warriors and twenty-seven Rangers under Brant defeated their pursuers in a day-long battle. The Americans had 102 casualties out of a force of 149.

Early in July, a contingent from Niagara destroyed the settlement at Wilkes-Barre in Pennsylvania. John Butler, who led the raid, reported taking 227 scalps and only five prisoners. In September a large party of Indians, loyalists, and 'vagabond Canadians' raided the German Flats on the Mohawk, destroyed the crops and drove the cattle off towards Niagara. In November there was the bloody assault on Cherry Valley near Schenectady, in the hill country fifty miles from Albany. The rebel colonists clamoured that something should be done to protect the outposts of civilisation.

Washington's reaction to this demand was to plan a punitive expedition, the object of which was the 'total destruction and devastation of their settlements'. The Indian country was not merely to be overrun, but destroyed. The task was entrusted to General John Sullivan, who was ordered to capture as many prisoners as possible and to drive the remaining Indians into the hands of the British, where it was hoped they would create grave embarrassment.

The summer of 1778 had yielded a poor harvest, and the following winter proved disastrous to the imprudent Iroquois. The British were forced to feed them from supplies brought to Niagara from Quebec with much difficulty, and the commandant was told that if his Indians were hungry they should raid the Mohawk valley. Firearms and ammunition were in short supply and Butler reported that 'the Indians from the scarcity of provisions consume more of it than ordinary by firing at every little bird they see'. Washington, well aware of the Indian's plight, intended to defeat them not by winning battles, but by 'invoking the aid of war's ancient ally famine'.

The plan was for General Sullivan, with 2,500 men including Oneida scouts, to march from Wyoming along the Susquehanna River to Tioga, where he was to meet General James Clinton with 1,500 New Yorkers from Albany. A third force of 600 men under Colonel Daniel Brodhead was to march north along the Allegheny River from Fort Pitt, to meet the others somewhere in the Indian homeland in the Genesee country, but in fact it was forced to return. The British were soon informed of the enemy's movements by the Butlers, who moved about the Lake country organising the Indians in the defence of their villages.

On 22 August the junction at Tioga was successfully accomplished and three days later the combined forces made their first foray against the important Indian village of Chemung. They could not have timed things better, since the vegetables were already gathered and the corn was ready for harvesting. After all had eaten their fill the village and a large supply of corn was burned.

On the 29th the Americans attacked the village of Newtown

defended by about 1,000 warriors under Joseph Brant, and 250 Rangers and fifteen Regulars under John Butler. Unaccustomed to the canister fired at them by the Americans, the Indians fled, leaving eleven dead, who were promptly scalped by the attackers. Two of them were skinned from the hips down to provide leggings for two American officers. Although small, Newtown was one of the most decisive engagements of the revolution, for after it the terrified Indians would never face the invaders in battle. The unhappy fate of the great Iroquois Confederacy was decided on that August day.

After some unsuccessful skirmishing and attempts to ambush the Americans in the Genesee country, the outnumbered Indians and loyalists fled westward to Niagara, leaving the Americans to lay waste the Genesee country and the Mohawk at their leisure. When the campaign was over Sullivan, with a loss of fewer than forty men, had destroyed forty villages, 160,000 bushels of corn and a vast quantity of other vegetables; in one place his men destroyed 1,500 peach trees. That winter between two and three thousand Indians gathered at Niagara suffering cruelly from cold, hunger, and scurvy.

If Washington thought he had put an end to the Indian menace on the frontier, he was mistaken for the raiding bands returned early in 1780. In March a band of some 100 Indians surprised the small garrison at Skenesborough, destroyed the buildings, scalped a man and his wife, and retired to Canada with sixteen prisoners. In May, Sir John Johnson with 400 soldiers and 200 Indians returned to Johnson Hall in the Mohawk valley, destroying the neighbouring area. All summer hostile parties made lightning raids, massacred, pillaged and burned before retiring swiftly, so keeping the troops on the alert and making it necessary to call out the militia time and again.

On 2 August Joseph Brant swooped down on the unsuspecting Canajoharie settlement, and his force killed seventeen people, took forty-one prisoners, destroyed all the cattle, burnt fifty-two houses, forty-two barns, a church, and a grist mill. In September Sir John Johnson, with 750 picked men of the 20th and 34th regiments, together with some Hessian jägers, Butler's Rangers and Brant and his Mohawks, made another prolonged raid into the Mohawk valley, during which 200 or so buildings were burned and 150,000 bushels of wheat destroyed. At the same time Major Christopher Carleton with 1,500 soldiers and Indians came down Lake Champlain to capture Fort Edward, ravaging the Ballston area on the way. These raids, prompted by hunger as well as revenge, left the once fertile Mohawk valley in ruins.

To the west and south the pattern of Indian raids, inspired and encouraged by loyalists, was repeated. The Delawares and the Shawnees waged a bloody war on the borders of Pennsylvania and Virginia, until, in 1778, a small force of 200 Americans under General Clarke conquered southern Illinois in a punitive expedition. On 17 September the Delawares signed a peace treaty with the United States, but the battles between the Shawnees and the Virginians continued.

In 1781 the Cherokees became restless and made incursions into South Carolina, but General Pickens stormed through their country, with a hastily mustered body of 400 horsemen, killing forty Indians and destroying thirteen villages. Farther south, George Hanger saw 600 Cherokee and Creek Indians, near Savannah, preparing and training for war:

> The Indians abstain from women, take physic, and prepare their bodies for war, by frequently running, and using other manly exercises. In one, not unlike the game we call *goff*, they shew great skill and activity. They were a very fine race of men. One of their Chiefs came to pay his respect to the Commanding Officer at Savannah. . . .
> He was mounted on a small, mean Chichesaw horse, about twelve hands and a half high; his dress consisted of a linen shirt, a pair of blue cloth trowsers, with yellow and scarlet down the outward seam; over this he had on an old full-dress uniform of the English foot-guards, the lace very much tarnished; a very large tye-wig on his head; an old gold-laced uniform hat, Cumberland-cocked; a large gorget round his neck, a sword in a belt, hung over his shoulder; a tomahawk and scalping-knife in his girdle; rings in his nose and ears; his face, and breast, which was quite open, painted various colours; and a musket on his shoulder. He was one of the most distinguished Chiefs amongst the whole Indian nations, and was called the *mad dog*. . . .

In 1782 these Creeks under their Chief Guristersigo struck at the American troops under General Anthony Wayne outside Savannah. The Americans although surprised rallied quickly and repulsed the

Indians with the loss of many warriors including the Chief, and from then on they gave no further trouble.

After the war Sir John Johnson devoted himself to helping the impoverished Indians and loyalists in Canada, later becoming Superintendent of Indian Affairs for British North America. The Mohawks, who according to Chief Brant had lost property to the value of £16,000 during the war, and the other Iroquois, together with some Delawares, settled in Canada along the banks of the Great River and never returned to their native valley.

Force of the Indian nations on the occurrence of the American Revolution

1.	**Iroquois**	
	Mohawks	100
	Oneidas and Tuscaroras	400
	Onondagas	230
	Cayugas	220
	Senecas	650
		1,600
2.	**Iroquois of the West**	
	Wyandots	180
	Total Iroquois	1,780
3.	**Algonquins**	
	Ottowas	450
	Chippewas	5,000
	Mississagies	250
	Pottawattamies	450
	Miamies	300
	Piankashaws ⎫	800
	Weas, under the name of ⎬	
	Musketoons, &c. ⎭	
	Monomonies	2,000
	Shawnees	300
	Delawares ⎫	600
	Munsees ⎬	
	Total Algonquins	10,150

4. **Dakotas**
   Sioux 500

5. **Appalachians**
   Cherokees 500
   Chickasaws 150
   Choctaws 900
   Catawbas 150
   Natchez } Alabamas 600
   Muscogees } Cowetas 700

   Total Appalachians 3,000

   Total Indian Forces 15,430

THE CONTINENTAL ARMY

The charters of the Royal Provinces of North America had from the earliest times provided for the creation of a militia, while a similar authority was assumed by the non-royal colonies. In addition volunteer, or independent companies, were formed in the more thickly populated areas by the wealthier citizens. In time of war active service units were recruited and usually engaged for one year's service, although attempts were made to retain them for longer periods by offering extra pay and other inducements.

After the capture of Louisberg in 1744, Governors Pepperill and Shirley were each authorised to raise a regiment of infantry from the colonists who had taken part in the expedition, to be maintained as a regular British regiment. In 1756 the Royal American Regiment was raised in Pennsylvania to guard the eastern frontier. It was composed largely of Germans, many of whom came direct from Germany and Switzerland. Later, when major operations were undertaken against the French and Indians, regular British units began to be sent out, while the colonies provided militia, volunteers and rangers. These last were hunters and frontiersmen, who furnished their own arms and equipment, and were organised into companies of 100 men.

The expulsion of the French from Canada during the Seven Years War had been just such a combined effort, but in the subsequent Indian rising support from the colonists had been meagre and grudging. The burden of the fighting had fallen on the British regulars. This prompted the British government to propose the quartering of 10,000 troops permanently in North America, to be paid for in whole or in part by the colonists in the form of increased taxation. With their ingrained distrust of standing armies, the Americans found this to be one of their principal grievances. Nevertheless, when the occasion arose such as in New York, in 1766 and 1770 in Pennsylvania, they were prepared to ask for the aid of British troops in settling internal disputes over land and boundaries. The threat of an attack from Spain in 1771 created an upsurge of loyalty which increased the recruiting figures in America, but this was short-lived.

A new Militia Law of 1775 provided for the enrolment of all free males between the ages of sixteen and fifty. They were formed into companies and regiments, commanded by officers appointed by the Governor. They were required to turn out for periodic inspections and drills, which in fact were seldom held, armed with a musket or rifle, bayonet, sword, or tomahawk, brush and picker, pouch or cartouche box, flints, pack, blanket, and canteen or water-bottle. They were engaged to serve, without pay, for short periods within the borders of their own states. The numbers of men that could be raised by this system were considerable. For instance, in 1774 Connecticut possessed some 26,000 militiamen, while, in the following year, New Jersey had twenty-six regiments of infantry and eleven troops of cavalry, and Pennsylvania fifty-three battalions of infantry.

In 1769, six years before the outbreak of the revolution, the 'Baron' de Kalb, was sent to America by the French Marshal Broglie to report on the colonists' preparedness for open warfare. They had, he noted, facilities for creating a large merchant marine, and although there were neither arsenals nor magazines, yet they were plentifully supplied with cannon. Merchants carried stocks of powder for sale to the Indians, and the inhabitants were well supplied with firearms. The large rivers would enable them to supply considerable armies by boat. The forts in the interior were in a bad state, and those on the coast were of little use. Finally he estimated that there were 200,000 young men enrolled in the militia who could be called out without disturbing the necessary civilian occupations. By the end of the war in 1783, some 164,087 militiamen had passed through the ranks of the American armies, confirming the Baron's estimate.

The opening action of the American revolution, the march of the British from Boston to Lexington and Concord to destroy rebel stores, was opposed by armed citizens formed into 'Alarm' companies of 'Minute-men', or militiamen selected to be ready at a moment's notice. Within weeks of the news of this engagement the New England states, led by Massachusetts, managed to assemble an army for the siege of the British in Boston.

In June 1775 the Continental Congress, in session at Philadelphia, passed three important resolutions. The first was to adopt and take over the New England army around Boston as a 'Continental' force. The second was to appoint George Washington of Virginia 'General and Commander-in-Chief of all the Continental forces raised, or to be raised, for the defence of American Liberty'. The third was to adopt a code of 'Rules and Regulations for the government of the

Army'. Armed with the latter Washington took over command at Cambridge on 2 July 1775. On paper his army was 20,000 strong but only 17,000, three-quarters of whom were from Massachusetts, and the rest from New Hampshire, Connecticut and Rhode Island, were present and fit for duty.

The task of welding this motley assembly into a regular army was immense. The 'battalions' and 'regiments' were of different sizes and establishments, deficient in discipline, instruction, arms and ammunition, and in every other military essential. They were enlisted for the rest of that year only, their company officers had been enlisted by themselves, their field officers by the company officers, and the general officers by Congress. The overriding qualification for rank seems to have been an ability to raise men, and those who could provide fifty men became captains and 500 colonels. Authorities differ as to how many had seen service before. British historians generally maintain that many had served in the French and Indian wars, and American historians that the number of such veterans were few. All, however, are agreed that it was a crude and ragged host, in which intoxication, peculation, falsification of returns, disobedience of orders and disrespect to officers were common offences. To stamp out these vices, all the draconian disciplinary measures found in the armies of the European princes, such as the pillory, the wooden horse, drumming out and whipping, were applied. The New England contingents were soon joined by others from New York, and, even farther afield, from the borders of Pennsylvania and Virginia, where discipline was little better. From such unpromising materials Washington created an army, and in spite of almost annual reorganisations caused by the short terms of enlistment, managed to keep it together for seven years.

At the close of 1775, the term of service of the New England army came to an end, while it was still besieging Boston, but by hook and by crook Washington managed to disband it and raise another 'within distance of a reinforced enemy'. By February he was once more in command of nearly 18,000 men, with the cannon taken at Ticonderoga and with sufficient ammunition to drive the British from Boston. In spite of the obvious disadvantages of such a system, Washington was unable (in the words of Fortescue), to 'induce the lawyers and praters at Philadelphia to sanction the making of an American New Model Army', and in the autumn of 1776, while retreating through New Jersey with a discouraged and despondent force, he had to repeat the same operation. The fact that he was also able to launch an operation as successful as that which surprised the Hessians at Trenton is a striking indication of his abilities.

For the year 1777 he proposed to Congress the formation of a standing army for the duration of the war. After much discussion Congress agreed to vote an army of 66,000 men for three years or the duration, authorising Washington to raise 15,000 more if he thought fit, and extending his powers as commander-in-chief. It was decided that the army of the states should comprise eighty-three battalions. The states were to clothe and arm these troops, and select their officers, while Congress would commission and pay the officers, and maintain the army. In fact actual enlistments did not equal the number of men authorised, and as it was impossible to get the recruits to agree on a term of enlistment no fixed period was set. Some men enlisted for three years, some for nine months, and others for only three months.

This new 'Continental' army, recruited during the winter and spring at Morristown, numbered barely 15,000, divided into five divisions, ten brigades, and forty-three 'regiments' or 'battalions'. It fought through the campaign of 1777 in Pennsylvania, suffering defeat at Brandywine and Germantown, and in the winter of 1777 retired to Valley Forge. Throughout this period the army under Washington was usually referred to as the 'Main army', as opposed to the 'Northern army', formed in Canada in 1775, and the 'Southern army', which could be said to date from February 1776, when a staff was created to command the troops in the service of Congress in the Southern Department.

Throughout the long winter of 1777–1778, the Continental army, now less than 3,000 strong, half-naked and half-starved, suffered terribly from cold, famine, and sickness. By Christmas they were driven into open mutiny, and were on the point of disbanding when, early in 1778, news was received of the treaty with France. Immediately enthusiasm returned, recruiting revived, and the efficiency of the army increased. Much of the improvement was attributable to Washington's drill-master, the German Baron v. Steuben. He regulated the size and organisation of the battalions, dividing any 'regiment' of over 320 men into two battalions, laying down that no battalion was to have less than 160 privates, and established a regulation system of drill to take the place of the various British textbooks then in use, such as Bland's *A treatise of Military Discipline,* and

Simes' *The Military Guide for Young Officers*. In May 1778 Congress adopted a new establishment for the battalion of eight companies of fifty-three men and a Light Company, which was usually detached to the corps of light infantry.

When the Continental army set off in pursuit of the British in June 1778, and overtook them at Monmouth, it was probably in a higher state of discipline and efficiency than at any other time during the war. By January 1781, however, the army was at a low ebb again and the men of the Pennsylvania and New Jersey brigades, grown tired of service, mutinied, killed their officers and elected leaders from the ranks. Lack of pay was one of their main grievances and there was equal danger of their marching upon Philadelphia and extorting payment from Congress by force, or of joining the British. Washington sent General Knox to the Governors of the various New England states to tell them about the mutiny and to request supplies of money and clothing to prevent other contingents following suit. The Continental army was short of men, money, rations, and clothing, and it was only the moral and practical aid of the French contingent which enabled Washington to resume the offensive. Marching rapidly from Connecticut to Virginia he surrounded Cornwallis at Yorktown, captured his army, and put an end to the military operations of the war. The objects of the Revolution – the defeat of the British army and the establishment of American independence – had been achieved by what was in effect an irregular army composed of successive relays of untrained recruits. 231,771 continentals and 164,087 militia, totalling 395,858, were called out for service during the war.

The bulk of the American infantry was equivalent to the common line infantry of the European armies. There are hints that some regiments had grenadier companies, but they must have been extremely rare, and hardly anything is known about them. Light infantry companies, as we have seen, were introduced in May 1778. The normal tactical unit, the battalion, varied considerably in size throughout the war. Regiments normally consisted of one battalion, although excessively small regiments were sometimes formed into composite battalions, and equally rarely large regiments were formed into two battalions. The normal strength of the battalion would seem to have been about 250 officers and men. Brigades, formed from two to six battalions, usually came from the same state.

Although Washington was fully alive to the use and value of the mounted arm, shortage of money, horses and saddlery, kept Continental cavalry formations to a minimum. Although Congress, in November 1776, directed its cavalry committee to raise and arm 3,000 horsemen, the number actually raised does not seem to have exceeded 1,000.

The Americans had several 'legions' of combined horse and foot. The modern legion had been first proposed by Marshal Saxe, who based his idea upon a study of the Roman legion. France, Prussia, and Austria all used legions during the Seven Years War, and it was here that v. Steuben saw them, later recommending their use to Washington.

Apart from those officers who were in a position to provide themselves with suits of regimentals, the American militia wore their ordinary clothes, and that was how they were dressed at Lexington and Concord. The New England army at Boston does not seem to have had a much more military appearance, since, as one observer put it, they seemed 'most wretchedly clothed, and as dirty a set of mortals as ever disgraced the name of a soldier'.

When the revolution started, industries such as textiles were in their infancy and, with the British navy restricting trade, there was a severe shortage of clothing, blankets, woollen and cotton goods. This situation made the clothing of the Continental army a permanent problem for Washington. Supplies were eked out by imports from France, and by thinly disguised captured British uniforms. The acceptance of orders from Congress was hazardous, both physically and financially. For example, a Mr Ross, ordered to furnish 30,000 yards of blue and brown broadcloth, with 3,000 yards of various coloured fancy cloth for facings, was forbidden to purchase anywhere in Great Britain or Ireland, and was advised to consign his goods to Martinique, St Eustatius, or Curaçao, to avoid seizure by British cruisers. After all this trouble to obtain the goods which Congress required he had no guarantee that he would ever be paid.

On 4 November 1775 Congress adopted brown, already popular with the New England Provincials, as the first official colour of the Continental army. The various regiments were to be distinguished by different colour collars, cuffs, and lapels. The cut of the coats was similar to that of the British, but plainer, with worked, instead of laced, button-holes. Cocked hats with a black cockade, white or buff waistcoats and breeches, and 'half-spatterdashes' completed the regulation dress. In fact some of the earlier organisations had already chosen their uniforms, and brown was by no means universally adopted. Washington hoped to have the Continental army all in uniform by the beginning of 1776, but he was only partially successful, and after a few months of work in the trenches before New York the uniforms already issued were worn out. It is apparent from a study of the numerous descriptions of deserters from the Continental army, quoted by Lefferts and others, that a complete uniform was the exception rather than the rule.

In the spring of 1778, after the disastrous winter at Valley Forge, a shipment of blue and brown coats was received from France and the newly trained Continental army must have made a brave appearance. After a year of campaigning, however, they were once again in rags. On 2 October 1779 Washington issued a General Order which formed the basis for the first American dress regulations. The infantry were to be clothed in dark blue, with different facings and distinctions for groups of states. The army was not clothed at once according to this order but only as supplies permitted, and as before it varied sharply from comparative smartness to near-nakedness. At the same time that the Pennsylvania and New Jersey brigades were in open mutiny, the French noted with astonishment the handsome show the Americans made, 'well clothed and drilling superbly'. A year later, however, General Greene was complaining that his men were 'almost naked for want of overalls and shirts, and the greater part of the army barefoot'.

If conventional European military clothing was scarce, the Americans had their own substitute, which was in certain respects superior and ready to hand. This was the hunting dress worn by the frontiersmen of Pennsylvania and Virginia, derived from Indian clothing, and consisting generally of an unbleached homespun or deerskin shirt, or 'frock', fringed deerskin leggings and moccasins. Washington who thought this style of dress cheap, clean, light, adaptable and flexible, requested 10,000 sets to be furnished for the army:

> If I were left to my own inclination, I should not only order
> the men to adopt the Indian dress, but cause the officers
> to do it also, and be the first to set the example myself.

Congress included rifle frocks in the clothing bounty given to the rank and file, and the states also supplied them to their troops, for wear as working dress or as a substitute when coats were unavailable. Their use became so general, however, that to all intents and purposes they became the service dress of the American army, and as such may be said to be America's contribution to the development of military dress.

The bulk of the American infantry carried smoothbore flintlock muskets, the standard weapon being the British 'Brown Bess'. The colonists had to get their weapons wherever they could with the result that many different types and sizes were in use at the same time. France shipped 30,000 muskets to America in 1777, which, drawn from army reserves, were mainly of the 1763 pattern, although some were as old as 1717, and some as new as 1777. The West Indies and Holland were other sources of supply, while General Lee even managed to get some from Prussia, which unfortunately turned out to be useless government rejects.

To overcome differences in calibre the various brigades of the army tried unsuccessfully to standardise by exchanging weapons. At Brandywine, according to General Lee, no single brigade had muskets of uniform calibre, which made the exchange of ammunition in battle impractical, with disastrous results. At Valley Forge v. Steuben noted that 'muskets, carbines, fowling pieces and rifles were found in the same company'.

Much has been written of the devastating effects of the American rifle. The rifle was introduced to the colonies about 1700 by German and Swiss emigrants, and in the hands of American gunsmiths did indeed develop into an extremely accurate weapon. Although fine performances could be obtained by individuals, however, 150 yards (137 m) seems to have been the maximum range 'otherwise their fire is not effective'. In addition the rifle had several serious disadvantages. Riflemen were to be found only on the western borders of Pennsylvania and the colonies to the south, and the accurate American rifle existed only in limited numbers. Moreover it took three times as long to load as a smoothbore musket, and was more liable to be put out of action by bad weather conditions. The rifle was not equipped with a bayonet so that the rifleman could neither stand nor give a charge and was consequently useless in the line of battle. The number of rifles used in the Continental army was gradually reduced until by 1781 they were 'generally disused'.

The American soldier carried some thirty rounds made up into cartridges by himself, upon his person, but there was a chronic shortage of good waterproof leather cartouche boxes. V. Steuben was struck by the fact the Americans were compelled to carry their powder in pouches and cows' horns as only a few had good boxes. To remedy this shortage Washington introduced tin canisters which contained thirty-six cartridges. The situation was so serious that on one occasion, when it rained heavily during an engagement, the Americans had to retire because their powder was wet. The militia, as a rule, did not use cartridges, carrying their powder in special horns, and their rounds in leather ball-bags.

The short range of the musket, and the constant danger of misfire in adverse weather conditions, made the use of the bayonet the hallmark of well-trained and disciplined troops, but at first the Americans had no faith in cold steel. As the war progressed, however, and the Continentals received more training and battle experience, so they made increased use of the bayonet. In 1799 Stony Point was taken by the corps of light infantry by a brilliant assault, with bayonets fixed and muskets unloaded, and they repeated the performance at the redoubt at Yorktown. As American muskets were of different makes and sizes, the bayonets had to be made individually to fit each weapon.

For the rest, officers up to and including captain carried swords and espontoons, or half-pikes, and Chastellux, describing the light infantry in 1780, noted that the officers had espontoons, and the 'subalterns' had 'fusils'. Sergeants were armed with musket and bayonet, although they might have a short sword or hanger.

There is no doubt that very few Americans knew anything of the proper employment of artillery. Henry Knox, who was to command the artillery in the Continental army, and a few others, gained their early training in the Boston Train of Artillery, which had practised with both siege and field pieces under British instructors. Elsewhere there seems to have been little in the way of practical experience, although organisations existed in the larger coastal towns such as Charleston, Philadelphia and New York. The Continental artillery disgraced itself at Bunker Hill, under the Gridleys, but 'no guns were better handled' at Trenton, Princeton and Monmouth, under Kno. In fact it was largely due to his zeal that the Continental artillery reached a peak of efficiency as quickly as it did.

The general characteristics of artillery weapons and their performance have already been described under the British army. Some fifty assorted pieces of artillery had been assembled by the New England army besieging Boston before Washington took over command. Under the direction of Knox, a further sixty odd pieces captured at Ticonderoga were hauled overland to Cambridge during the winter of 1775–1776, and another seventy were left behind when the British evacuated Boston. Most of the field pieces in the hands of the Continental army were small naval guns, either found in store or captured at sea. Apart from two Müller brass 3-pounders, the property of the Boston Regiment since 1762 and used by the Continental artillery throughout the war, most of the guns were obsolete iron pieces.

Other pieces were captured, from the British at Saratoga and the Hessians at Princeton, some were imported from France, and others including some brass pieces were cast in New York and Pennsylvania. The French pieces, consisting mainly of 4-pounders with a few 8-pounders were sent out with only a few Gribeauval carriages, and were mounted on American copies of the British Müller carriage. After v. Steuben's reorganisation of the Continental army at Valley Forge each battalion was supposed to have two 'grasshopper' guns, swivel guns mounted on wooden cradles which could be carried by two men.

The American revolution was a war of skirmishers. Few of Washington's troops, it has been said, could manoeuvre in the open, and fewer ventured to cross bayonets with the British regulars. They could not fire volleys in the disciplined manner of European troops, but they fired at will, aiming at the target. 'There were no great battles', the German General v. Bulow wrote, 'it was a war of light troops. The manoeuvres of the American General at Trenton and Princeton were masterpieces. They may be deemed models for the conduct of a general supporting a defensive war against a superior enemy'. As to the action of Yorktown which ended the war, it must, he thought, 'have occurred to every mind'. Indeed, at the moment of its final triumph, the American revolution was on the eve of collapse, and it was to the blunders of the British, both naval and military, rather than to the prowess of the Continental army, that the successful outcome of the war was due.

6

THE FRENCH ARMY

The French, smarting from their defeat in the Seven Years War, viewed Britain's disputes with her American colonies with a good deal of satisfaction. While outwardly friendly they were, in Fortescue's words, 'full of enmity and malice'. In 1769 Marshal de Broglie sent the 'Baron' de Kalb to North America to report on the developing war situation there, in which he hoped to have a command, and when the revolution broke out France provided considerable material support. In 1776 the American agent in Paris, Silas Deane, obtained as gifts 30,000 stand of arms, as many uniforms, 250 pieces of artillery and vast quantities of military stores. In addition, American privateers could always be sure of a welcome in French ports where they were sheltered, provisioned and allowed to sell their prizes. The Caribbean swarmed with French privateers masquerading under American colours.

The American cause soon became the rage at the French court and many aristocrats rushed to America to offer their services to Washington. As Talleyrand wrote, 'Old military men saw in it a war, the young men something new, the women something adventurous'. In general the volunteers were not much use with the exception of the young Marquis de Lafayette, who fought through the Pennsylvania campaign and proved himself a good and energetic soldier.

After Saratoga France's enmity came out into the open. She concluded a treaty with the colonists and secretly despatched the Toulon squadron under Vice-Admiral the Comte d'Estaing with 4,000 troops to America, where he appeared on 8 July off the mouth of the Delaware. For the first time during the war Britain's vital supremacy at sea was threatened. After the abortive expedition to Rhode Island d'Estaing took his troops to the West Indies and it was here, at St Lucia, that the first military contest between the British and the French took place.

Through the whole of 1779, France, now allied with Spain, planned a descent on the English coast, and it was only when this venture failed that another expedition to America was prepared. The Marquis de Lafayette, who was then in France seeking aid for Washington, hoped to return at the head of a French expeditionary force, but on 1 March 1780 the command was given to Lieutenant-General the Comte de Rochambeau. With his commission he received the King's *Instructions*, which were to entrust the overall command of the troops to Washington, who was to be accorded the same honours as a Marshal of France. All plans of campaign were to be directed by the American General, and the French, as auxiliaries, were to give their allies precedence. In a secret rider, however, Rochambeau was told that there was to be no dispersal of the French troops, and that they were always to serve as an army corps under French generals.

His force was to consist of the Bourbonnois, Royal Deuxponts, Soissonois, Saintonge, Neustrie and Anholt infantry regiments, 900 men of the Lauzun Legion, a battalion of artillery, a company of bombardiers, some miners and workers with siege equipment – a force of some 8,000 men. On arrival at Brest, however, there were not enough ships available, so Rochambeau was forced to sail in two divisions, leaving the Neustrie and Anholt regiments, 300 men of Lauzun's Legion and part of the artillery to follow on later. The remainder totalled some 5,000 men. Sailing on 2 May, the French fleet reached Newport, Rhode Island, on 11 July, where the troops were encamped for nearly a year waiting for the arrival of the second division. On 10 June 1781 Rochambeau left Newport and joined Washington near White Plains where they concerted plans for an attack on New York. While they were making their plans news came that Cornwallis had entrenched himself at Yorktown, and that answering a call for aid Admiral de Grasse was bound for the Chesapeake, with twenty-nine ships and 3,000 men of the Gâtinois, Agenois, and Touraine regiments under the command of the Marquis de Saint-Simon. The combined armies immediately marched south. On 3 September the French paraded through Philadelphia, and eleven days later they were at Williamsburg, where they found that Lafayette commanding an American force together with Saint-Simon had already bottled Cornwallis up in Yorktown.

The French contingent took an active part in the subsequent siege, and on 19 October, the British garrison marched out between two lines of the enemy, the Americans on one side, and the French on the other. After Yorktown the French saw no more fighting in North America, and in January 1783 Rochambeau returned to France.

The brilliant and indisciplined French army had come out of the

Seven Years War demoralised but by 1775, under the reforming guidance of de Choiseuil and his successor Saint-Germain it had become the best equipped and trained that France had ever possessed. The bulk of the army in 1776, consisted, apart from a distinguished *Maison du Roi*, of 112 infantry regiments. Like the British, the French had their recruiting difficulties and of these regiments twenty-two were foreign, nine Swiss, three Irish, and two Italian, and the rest German. While they were difficult to discipline and prone to desertion in peacetime, the fighting record of the foreign regiments was excellent. Each regiment consisted of two battalions of four companies, with a grenadier and light infantry company, or *chasseurs*, to each regiment. Each company was subdivided into two platoons or four sections.

In addition to the line regiments, which all had princely or territorial titles as well as their numbers, there was a whole assortment of light troops. These were originally formed from the numerous grooms and servants accompanying the French army during the War of the Austrian Succession, to protect the baggage from the enemy's hussars and pandours. They proved effective and after the war were increased, at the instigation of Marshal Saxe, by selecting suitable officers from the infantry and putting them in command of mixed companies of volunteers. De Grassin and de la Morlière were two infantry officers who became notable leaders of units of this kind.

After the War of the Austrian Succession it began to dawn on French military theorists that the success achieved by Frederick the Great and his troops was not brought about by good luck, but had some direct connection with the so-called 'Prussian order' – their characteristic rapid fire, cadenced step and wide deployment in line. For more than fifteen years, from 1749–1778, the question of which was superior, the French order in column (*l'ordre profond*), or the Prussian order in line (*l'ordre mince*), was the subject of frequent debate. The advocates of the former, headed by the Marshal de Broglie, held that it was the natural order for Frenchmen, and that it was only by adhering to it faithfully that Turenne and his disciples had gained their greatest successes. The supporters of the latter, whose spokesman was the theorist Guibert, replied simply that it was necessary to keep up with the changing face of warfare. In the time of the Emperor Maximilian ranks had been formed thirty to forty men deep; under Charles V, twenty to twenty-five deep; under

Gustavus Adolphus and Maurice of Nassau, ten deep; under Montecuculli, Conde, and Turenne, eight deep; at the beginning of the eighteenth century, five deep. Because the length of the musket would not permit three ranks to fire standing, Frederick the Great had invented the system of firing in three different postures with the front rank kneeling, which was a development soon to be widely adopted. In view of these constant changes, Guibert asked, how could one do otherwise than oppose an enemy in a formation approximating to his own? This discussion was cut short by Saint-Germain after a commission, of which Rochambeau was a member, had reported to him. The resulting regulations of 1776 and 1777 retained the French order for the purposes of forcing a point in the enemy's line, clearing an obstacle or passing a defile, but established the Prussian order as the regular and habitual fighting formation.

When Saint-Germain died and was succeeded by a conservative, the supporters of the 'Old School' tried to reverse the situation. In 1778 forty-four battalions of infantry and six regiments of dragoons assembled at Vaussieux in Normandy, prepared for an invasion of England. De Broglie, who commanded, planned to profit from the occasion by making a comparison of the two systems in the field, choosing Rochambeau to head the forces which would fight according to the new ideas. In spite of strenuous efforts de Broglie was worsted in all the movements he attempted in the French order, and was compelled to concede victory. As a result of Rochambeau's performance on this occasion he was given the command of the advance-guard of the invasion force, and, when that project was abandoned, the command of the American expedition.

The French cavalry consisted of the companies of the *Maison du Roi* and the *Gendarmerie de France*, and the line cavalry of horse, dragoons, and hussars. During the Seven Years War light mounted units had rendered great service and had developed at the expense of the dragoons, which were correspondingly reduced in number. Many of these light units, or 'legions', contained both cavalry and infantry. Of this kind was the *Voluntaires Etrangères de la Marine*, commanded by the Duc de Lauzun. Apart from the fifty dragoons which formed part of Saint-Simon's expeditionary force, the hussars of Lauzun's legion were the only French cavalry sent to America.

The *Règiment Royale-Artillerie*, numbered 47th and later 64th in the line, in fact consisted of seven regiments, each of two battalions of seven companies of gunners, two of bombardiers, and one of sappers, totalling some 12,000 men. Each regiment, which was based at and named after one of the following seven places – La Fére, Grenoble, Metz, Strasbourg, Besançon, Auxonne, and Toule – was a self-contained unit able to supply an army in the field with all the necessary gunners. Thanks to the Vallières, father and son, and to Jean Baptiste Gribeauval, great improvements had been made in the artillery. Until the arrival of Vallière *père* the artillery had remained in the state in which it had been left by Vauban, excellent for the leisurely siege warfare, favoured by Louis XIV, but totally unsuited, both in quantity and mobility for the Frederician warfare of quick marches and wide deployments. Vallière improved the service considerably by reducing the number of types of gun to five, making them shorter, lighter and more manageable, and by establishing special artillery schools, but the French artillery remained too heavy. In an attempt to rectify this fault an especially light 4-pounder, drawn by three horses and served by a small crew under a sergeant, was attached to each battalion, but the experiment was a failure; the guns impeded the movements of the infantry, and the inexperienced crew did not inspire much confidence in the infantrymen.

After the death of Vallière *fils* in 1776, Gribeauval, who had commanded the Austrian artillery during the Seven Years War, was entrusted by Saint-Germain with the task of reorganising the French artillery. Gribeauval's simple idea was to create special material for each artillery service, campaign, siege, fortress, and coastal, adapted for its particular task. The heavy 24- and 16-pounders were withdrawn from the field, relegated to siege work and replaced by newly designed 12-, 8- and 4-pounders, lighter than the old pieces of the same calibre. The gun carriages were made lighter and stronger with iron axle-trees and large diameter wheels. Henceforth wherever the army went, the artillery would be able to accompany and support it with its fire.

Other important innovations were the invention of wooden *sabots* and metal straps, by means of which the projectile could be attached to the cartridge; the introduction of strong, but light, waterproof ammunition wagons or *caissons*, which could carry spare ammunition alongside the guns; the introduction of the howitzer into the French service; improved sights and complete interchangeability of all parts made in the different arsenals. Surprisingly the one area where Gribeauval failed to alter the system was the provision of drivers, who continued to be hired civilians. The Prussians, who had introduced regular drivers at the time of the Great Elector and had possessed horse artillery from the beginning of the Seven Years War, were for some years to lead the field in these matters.

The infantry of the line wore the usual military clothing of the period, consisting of cocked hat, long-skirted coat, waistcoat, knee-length breeches, and gaiters which came up to above the knee. In the majority of French regiments the coat, waistcoat and breeches were of the traditional greyish-white, the colour of undyed wool. The regiments were distinguished by the colour of the collars, lapels and cuffs, the colour and arrangement of the buttons, and by the various shapes of the coat pockets. White gaiters were worn in summer and black in winter.

As in the British army the influence of Prussia made itself felt in the changes in the style of the uniform. As early as 1740 there had been a tendency to tighten up the cut of uniform to make it easier to perform the new close-order drill. In 1763 after the Seven Years War, a new uniform was introduced, based on the Prussian model, with a tight coat and small false cuffs and pocket flaps. It is believed that the corps commanded by Rochambeau wore uniforms of the 1767 pattern, since they had left France too soon to have received new uniforms following the regulations of 21 February 1779, by which the French infantry (with the exception of the royal regiment, the regiments of the princes, and the Picardie regiment), were divided into ten groups of six regiments. Each group, or division, had its own distinguishing colour as follows:

1–6	Sky blue	35–40	Primrose
7–12	Black	41–51	Crimson
15–19	Violet	52–62	Silver Grey
20–27	Steel Grey	70–72	Aurora (gold)
28–34	Rose	82–94	Dark Green

Each division was further divided into two groups of three regiments, the first of which had yellow metal buttons and horizontal pocket flaps, while the second group had white metal buttons and vertical pocket flaps. The three regiments in each group were distinguished by differences in the cuffs and lapels; the first regiment had lapels and cuffs of the group colour, the second, lapels and cuff piping, and the third, lapel piping and cuffs of the group colour. The pocket flaps in all cases were piped in the group colour, and the buttons bore the number of the regiment. This system illustrates the mania for uniformity which possessed the new reformer of the French army, and surpasses anything thought up by the Prussians.

By the regulations of 1779 the battalion companies, or *fusiliers*, wore hats with a white cockade, white shoulder straps piped in the group colour, and cloth skirt ornaments in the shape of a *fleur-de-lis*, also in the group colour. Grenadiers were deprived of their fur caps and given hats with a red pom-pom, red shoulder-straps piped in white, and cloth grenade on the skirts, together with chasseurs hats with a white cockade, green shoulder-straps piped in white and a cloth bugle horn on their skirts. The crested helmets displayed by some French infantry from 1772 were abolished in May 1776, but as the order stipulated that they were to be kept until they wore out, it is possible that some of the troops in the American expeditionary force used them although there is no confirmatory evidence.

Officers were distinguished by their gold or silver epaulettes and gilt gorgets, and in addition the French, unlike the British and Prussian armies, had a sophisticated system of rank markings. Non-commissioned officers were distinguished by rings of silver or blue lace round their cuffs. Of the foreign regiments, the Swiss and Irish wore red coats and the remainder sky-blue.

The regulations of 25 April 1767 specified a black leather car-touche box worn on a white buff shoulder-belt, and a waist-belt, fastening with a buckle for the swords and bayonets of the grena-diers and for the bayonets of the fusiliers, whose swords had been taken from them in 1764. The regulations of 2 September 1775 speci-fied a plate instead of a buckle for the waist-belt, and the flap of the cartouche box was to be cut square at the bottom. In 1776 the plate on the cartouche box was abolished, and the waist-belts were ordered to be worn over the shoulder. Finally on 21 February 1779 the fusiliers' bayonet-belt was abolished, and a frog was attached to the front of the cartouche box-belt.

The fur knapsack with two shoulder-straps was introduced after the Seven Years War during the ministry of Choiseuil, and was retained by the French army until after the Franco-Prussian War. In 1767, it was intended to contain two shirts, one stock, one pair of trousers, one pair of drawers, one pair of white gaiters for summer, one pair of black gaiters for winter, one pair of stockings, one pair of shoes, one box of combs, one pair of shoe brushes in a small bag, one tin box of blacking, one night cap, one forage cap and bread for four days. The infantryman also carried a linen haversack for rations, in which he could wrap himself at night, and a gourd-shaped water-bottle.

The *Maison du Roi*, the hussars, and the various light troops wore uniforms of a bewildering variety of colours, with different hats, *casques*, caps, and shakos. The horses were mainly dressed in cocked hats and blue coats, and the dragoons in green with helmets *a la Schomberg*. The artillery were dressed and equipped like the infantry but in blue with red facings, and blue waistcoats, and breeches.

The main infantry weapon was the flintlock musket and bayonet. After the War of the Spanish Succession the provision of arms ceased to be the responsibility of captains of companies, and passed to the state. From 1718, the royal factories of Charleville, Saint-Étienne, Mauberge and Klingenthal in Alsace started production, the last specialising in bladed weapons. The first model musket of 1717 was followed by numerous others. The second model of 1728 still had a wooden ramrod, but the introduction of iron ramrods into the Prussian army by Prince Leopold of Dessau was reflected in the 1746 model which was supplied with the new type. The 1763 model, which incorporated many improvements suggested by the earlier models, could already be considered as the definitive weapon. However, it was further improved in 1766, 1770, 1771 and 1774, until it finally appeared in 1777 in the form which was used through the revolution and Empire and which remained unchanged until the introduction of the percussion cap in 1842. The 1777 model weighed 9 lb 8 oz, (4·3 kilos), had a barrel length of 42 *Pouces* (1 m 37 cm) and iron furniture. The artillery pattern musket was slightly shorter. The new weapons were not issued immediately but were kept in store and only issued to regiments when their current arms were unservice-able. So the patterns issued from 1763–1777 would have been seen in use at the same time. The triangular-bladed bayonet came in a variety of models issued in 1763, 1766, 1768, 1774 and 1777. This last had a total length of 560 mm. The curved *sabre briquet* for grenadiers was introduced in 1770. The blade was 595·5 mm long. A regulation of 1 January 1766 stated that infantry officers were to be armed with 'uniform' fusils, bayonets, swords and cartouche boxes.

The short-lived experience of the French corps in America exerted a lasting influence on the French army. The activities of Lafayette in America and subsequently during the French revolution are well known. One of Rochambeau's aides-de-camp, Berthier, became Napoleon's chief-of-staff, and a Marshal of France, and Duportail, after his American service, became War Minister and was prominent in the subsequent reorganisation of the French army.

THE COLOUR PLATES

1. Aide-de-camp
   to a General Officer.

2. Lieutenant-General.

3. Adjutant-General.

4, 5, 6. Provincial Alarm Companies and Minutemen.

7. Grenadier, 43rd Regiment.

9. Sergeant, Grenadier Company, 18th or Royal Irish.

8. Officer, 23rd, or Royal Welch Fusiliers.

American Infantry

10. Militiaman.

12. Private, 4th Connecticut
Regiment of 1775.

11. Officer of Militia.

13. Sergeant, 5th Regiment.

14. Officer, 4th or King's Own.

15. Officer, 10th Regiment.

16. Private, Pennsylvania
    Rifle Regiment.

17. Officer, 1st Rhode
    Island Regiment.

18. Private Colonel Seth Warner's
    Battalion of Green Mountain
    Boys.

19. Private, Grenadier Company
    of Marines.

20. Officer, Battalion Company
    of Marines.

21. Gunner, Royal Regiment
    of Artillery.

22. Private, 4th Independent
    Maryland State Troops.

23. Officer, Colonel Sargent's
    Massachusetts Battalion.

24. Private, Colonel Patterson's
    Massachusetts Battalion.

25. Sergeant, Battalion Company, 52nd Regiment.

26. Pioneer, 59th Regiment.

27. Private, Battalion Company, 64th Regiment.

28. Gunner, Lamb's New
York Artillery Company.

29. Officer, Colonel Knox's
Artillery Regiment.

30. Gunner, Rhode Island
Train of Artillery.

British Infantry

31. Corporal, Battalion
Company, Marines.

32. Officer, Battalion
Company, 5th
Regiment.

33. Private, Battalion
Company, 38th
Regiment.

34. Aide-de-camp
    to a General Officer.

36. Brigadier-General.

35. Commander-in-Chief.

37. Sergeant, Battalion
Company, 1st Regiment.

38. Officer, Light Company,
Coldstream Regiment.

39. Private, Grenadier Company,
3rd Regiment.

40. Rifleman, 1st Regiment.

42. Sergeant, 6th Regiment.

41. Private, 12th Regiment.

43. Grenadier, 42nd Regiment.

44. Light Company Officer,
42nd Regiment.

45. Officer, 71st Regiment.

46. Private, 14th Regiment.

48. Private, 18th Regiment.

47. Officer, 8th Regiment.

49. Private, King's Royal
Regiment of New York.

51. Loyal American Association.

50. Officer, Queen's Rangers.

52. Private, 2nd New York
    Regiment.

53. Private, Light Company,
    2nd Canadian Regiment.

54. Private, 3rd New York
    Regiment.

55. Musketeer, Regiment v.
Trümbach.

56. Standard-bearer,
Fusilier Regiment v.
Ditfurth.

57. Grenadier Musketeer
Regiment Prinz Carl.

58. Private, Delaware
Regiment.

59. Officer, 2nd New
York Regiment.

60. Private, Maryland
Regiment.

61. Fusilier, Regiment
    Erbprinz.

62. Sergeant, Musketeer
    Regiment v. Donop.

63. Drummer, Musketeer
    Regiment v. Mirbach.

American Infantry

64. Private, 3rd New
    York Regiment.

66. Private, 1st Pennsylvania
    Battalion.

65. Officer, 3rd Pennsylvania
    Battalion.

67. Corporal, Fusilier
    Regiment v. Lossberg.

68. Officer, Musketeer
    Regiment v. Knyphausen.

69. Private, Grenadier
    Regiment v. Rall.

70. Corporal, 6th Virginia
    Regiment.

72. Sergeant, 7th Pennsylvania
    Regiment.

71. Private, 9th Pennsylvania
    Regiment.

73. Private, Garrison
    Regiment v. Huyn.

75. Pioneer, Garrison
    Regiment v. Stein.

74. Sergeant, Musketeer
    Regiment Wutginau.

76. Private, Colonel Lee's
    Regiment.

77. Private, Colonel Henley's
    Regiment.

78. Corporal, Colonel Hartley's
    Regiment.

79. Anspach-Bayreuth Gunner,
Artillery Company.

80. Hesse-Cassel Private,
Jäger Company.

81. Hesse-Cassel Gunner,
Artillery Company.

Additional Continental Regiments, 1777

82. Private, Colonel
    Webb's Regiment.

83. Officer, Colonel Sherburne's
    Regiment.

84. Private, Colonel Spencer's
    Regiment.

85. Private, Anhalt-Zerbsat
    Regiment.

86. Grenadier-Sergeant,
    2nd Brandenburg-Anspach
    Regiment.

87. Private, Waldeck 3rd
    Regiment.

88. Sergeant, 1st Continental
    Light Dragoons.

89. Officer, 3rd Continental
    Light Dragoons.

90. Dragoon, 16th Light
    Dragoons.

91. Officer, 17th Light
    Dragoons.

**American Infantry at
Valley Forge, 1777–1778**

92. Private, 13th Virginia
Regiment.

93. Sergeant, 1st Battalion
Philadelphia Associators.

94. Private, Light Infantry,
1st Battalion Philadelphia
Associators.

95. Bugler, 2nd Battalion,
    Light Infantry.

97. Private, Battalion Company,
    40th Regiment.

96. Officer, Light Infantry.

98. Corporal, 4th Connecticut
Regiment.

99. Private, Hall's Delaware
Regiment.

100. Private, 1st Connecticut
Regiment.

01. Grenadier, 21st Fusiliers.

103. Drummer, 34th Regiment.

102. Officer, Light Company,
53rd Regiment.

104. Lieutenant, 3rd Regiment.

106. Sergeant, 14th Regiment.

105. Lieutenant 8th Regiment.

107. Private, Battalion
Company, 9th Regiment.

108. Ensign, 24th Regiment.

109. Sergeant, Battalion Company,
47th Regiment.

Maryland Line

110. Private, 1st Regiment.

112. Corporal, 6th Regiment.

111. Sergeant, 2nd Regiment.

113. Gunner, Royal Artillery.

115. Sentry.

114. Private, Light Company,
62nd Regiment.

116. Private, 2nd New Hampshire
Regiment.

117. Private, 3rd New Jersey
Regiment.

118. Sergeant, 5th New York
Regiment.

119. Private, Butler's
     Rangers.

121. Private, Royal Highland
     Emigrants.

120. Loyalist Officer.

122. Private, State
Regiment.

123. Private, 5th Regiment.

124. Private, 11th
Regiment.

125. Dragoon, Regiment
Prinz Ludwig.

126. Officer, Jäger Company.

127. Sergeant, Light
Infantry Battalion
v. Barner.

128. Private, 2nd Virginia
Regiment.

129. Officer, 2nd Rhode Island
State Regiment.

130. Private, Virginia
State Line.

131. Sergeant, Regiment
v. Rhetz.

133. Private, Light Infantry,
Regiment v. Riedesel.

132. Officer, Regiment v. Specht.

134. Officer.

136. Private.

135. Officer, 5th Virginia
Regiment.

137. Grenadier, Brunswick Infantry
Regiment Prinz Friedrich.

138. Grenadier Sergeant, Hesse-Hanau
Infantry Regiment Erbprinz.

139. Gunner, Hesse-Hanau
Artillery Company.

American Troops

140. Canadian Winter Dress.

141. Officer, Continental Regiment of
Artillery Artificers.

142. Officer, Morgan's
Rifle Corps.

143. Red Jacket.

145. Warrior.

144. Joseph Brant.

146. Midshipman.

147. Captain.

148. Seaman.

149. Private, Pennsylvania
     State Marines.

150. Officer, Maryland
     State Marines.

151. Private, Continental
     Marines.

British Royal Navy

152. Captain, Full Dress.

153. Flag-officer, Undress.

154. Lieutenant.

155. Seaman.

156. Midshipman.

157. Seaman.

158. Captain, Full Dress.

160 Lieutenant, Full Dress.

159. Flag-officer, Full Dress.

French Royal Navy and Marines

161. Seaman.

162. Officer, Corps Royal de
l'Infanterie de la Marine.

163. Bombardier, Corps Royal
de l'Infanterie de la Marine.

164. Aide-de-camp to
a General Officer.

166. Brigadier-General.

165. Major-General.

167. Fifer, New Jersey
Regiments.

168. Sergeant, New York
Regiments.

169. Field Officer, New
Hampshire Regiments.

The Continental Army Regulations of 1779

170. Corporal, Delaware Regiments.

171. Captain, Pennsylvania Regiments.

172. Private, North Carolina Regiments.

173. Sergeant, Corps of
Continental Artillery.

174. Officer, Corps of Engineers.

175. Drummer, Corps of
Continental Artillery.

177. Officer, 2nd Regiment.

176. Dragoon, 4th Regiment.

179. Hussar, Queen's
Rangers.

178. Officer, British Legion.

180. Private, Pulaski's
Legion Infantry.

181. Officer, Armand's Legion.

182. Trooper, v. Heer's
Provost Corps.

183. Light Infantryman.

184. Grenadier.

185. Sergeant of Riflemen.

186. Private, 3rd North Carolina.

188. Private, 2nd South Carolina.

187. Officer, 1st South Carolina.

189. Private, North Carolina
    Volunteers.

190. Officer, 8th Regiment,
    Indian Dress.

191. Sergeant, 3rd Battalion,
    De Lancey's Brigade.

192. Private, Rhode Island
Light Infantry Company.

193. Officer, New York Light
Infantry Company.

194. Private, Massachusetts Light
Infantry Company.

195. Aide-de-camp to a General
Officer, Full Dress.

196. Lieutenant-General,
Full Dress.

197. War Commissary,
Full Dress.

198. Grenadier.

199. Hussar.

200. Corporal, Saintonge
Regiment.

201. Officer, Bourbonnois
Regiment.

202. Grenadier, Soissonois
Regiment.

French Troops

203. Gunner, Corps Royal
de l'Artillerie.

205. Officer of Grenadiers, Royal
Deux-Ponts Infantry Regiment.

204. Officer, Corps of Engineers.

206. Sergeant of Chasseurs,
Agenois Regiment.

207. Officer, Gatenois Regiment.

208. Grenadier, Touraine
Regiment.

209.

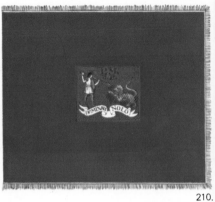

210.

211.

212.

213.

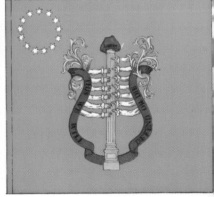

214.

215.

216.

217.

218.

219.

220.

221.

222.

223.

224.

225.

226.

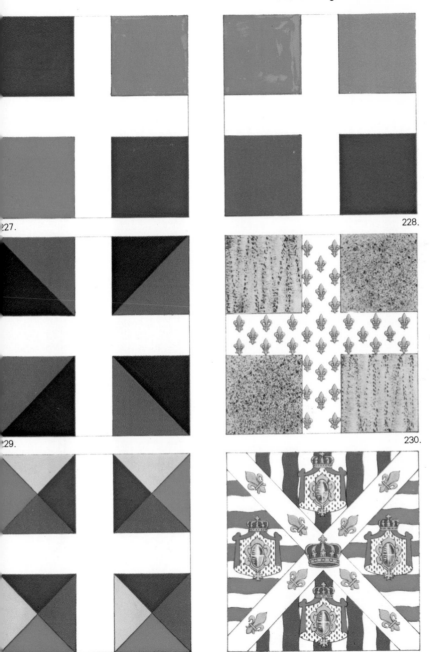

227.

228.

229.

230.

231.

232.

Firearms

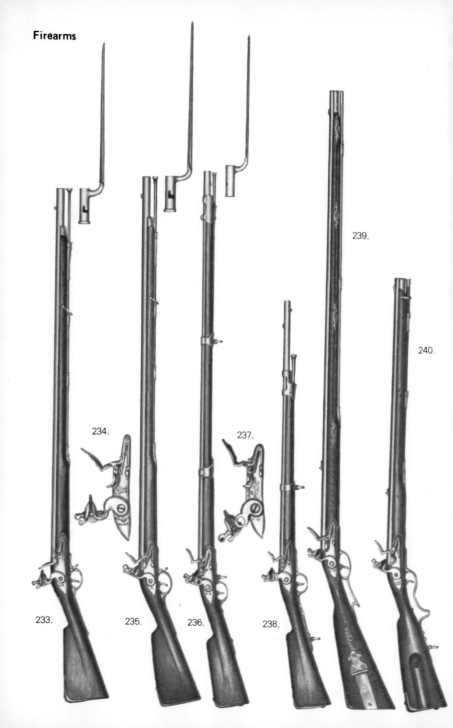

233.

234.

235.

236.

237.

238.

239.

240.

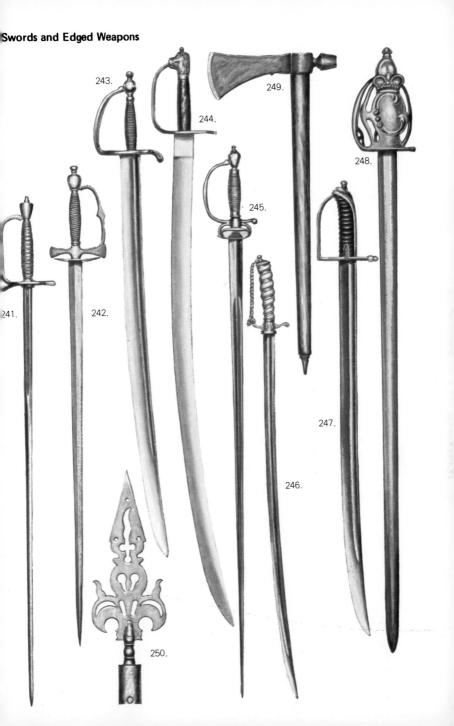

241.

242.

243.

244.

245.

246.

247.

248.

249.

250.

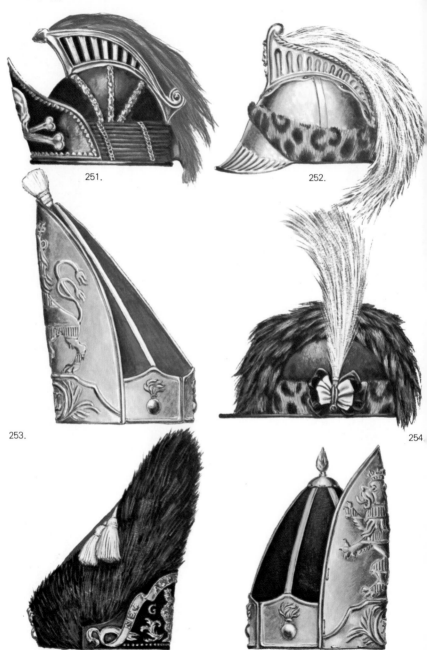

251.

252.

253.

254.

255.

256.

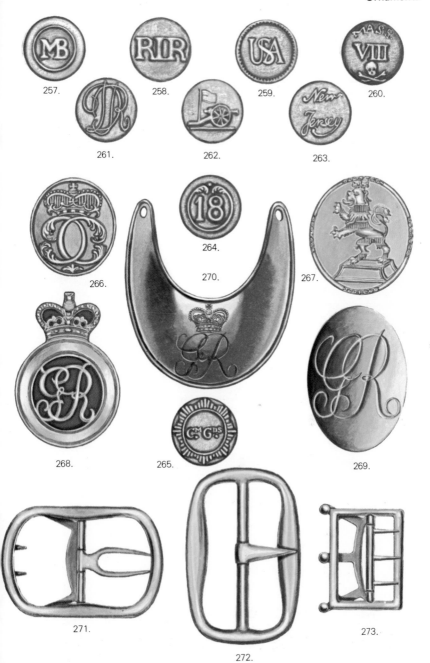

257.

258.

259.

260.

261.

262.

263.

266.

264.

270.

267.

268.

265.

269.

271.

272.

273.

British Infantry and Artillery Facings and Rank and File Lace

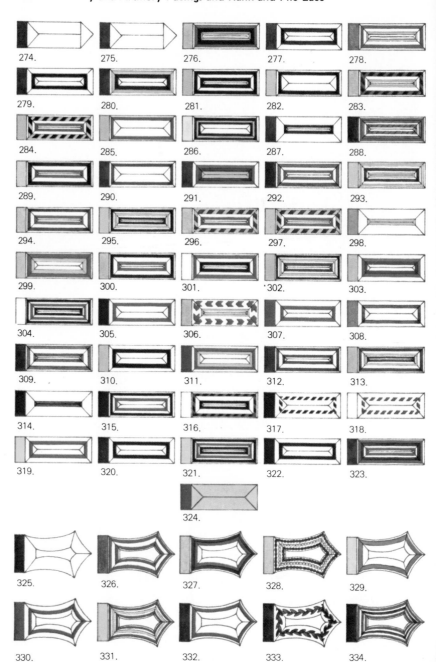

CAMPAIGNS AND PLATE DESCRIPTIONS

Boston, 1775

By the beginning of 1775 a force of British regulars, drawn from the garrisons scattered along the east coast of North America from Canada to Florida, was concentrated in the town of Boston under the command of General Gage, the Commander-in-Chief in North America. They were formed into three brigades as follows:

1st Brigade (Lord Percy)
4th Regiment
23rd Regiment
47th Regiment

2nd Brigade (Pigott)
5th Regiment
38th Regiment
52nd Regiment

3rd Brigade (Jones)
10th Regiment
43rd Regiment
59th Regiment
Detached companies of the 18th and 65th

Unattached
64th Regiment
Marines (two Battalions)

The flank companies of these regiments were massed together to form one composite battalion of grenadiers and one of light infantry.

On the night of 18 April 1775, a force consisting of some 800 men, formed from the grenadier and light infantry battalions under the command of Colonel Smith of the 10th Regiment, left Boston to march to the town of Concord, a distance of eighteen miles to seize rebel military stores. At daybreak on 19 April seventy 'Minutemen', warned of the British approach, assembled on Lexington Green. While they were being dispersed by the British vanguard there was firing and some eighteen casualties were inflicted on the rebels. During the morning the British reached Concord and began to destroy the rebel stores, but their pickets were so badly shot up by American marksmen that at noon Colonel Smith decided to return to Boston. As they left Concord, minutemen began to swarm on the British column from all sides. During the afternoon Smith and his exhausted troops were met by Lord Percy with 1,400 reinforcements at Lexington, and under constant rebel fire the combined force returned to Boston, which they reached at nightfall having suffered about 270 casualties. Colonel Smith's force consisted of the flank companies of the 4th, 5th, 10th, 23rd, 38th, 43rd, 47th, 52nd, 59th and Marines, the grenadier company of the 18th and a detachment of Royal Artillery.

After Lexington the hastily assembled New England army laid siege to

Boston which was surrounded by commanding hills. In an attempt to lift the siege in June, the British attacked the rebel position on Breed's or Bunker Hill, which they stormed with heavy casualties. The following regiments were engaged: thirteen companies of grenadiers, thirteen companies of light infantry, 5th, 38th, 43rd, 47th, 52nd, 1st Battalion Marines, Royal Artillery.

In March 1776 the Continental army occupied the commanding Dorchester Heights and the British evacuated the town of Boston, moving to Halifax.

The following order of battle, dated 16 July 1775, shows the organisation of the British troops at Boston after Bunker Hill.

Commander-in-Chief
Major-General Howe

	Major-General *Burgoyne* 2nd Bn. Arty.		*Major-General* *Clinton* 1st Bn. Arty.	
		Lt.-Col. *Cleveland*		

2nd Bde.	*4th Bde.*	*5th Bde.*	*3rd Bde.*	*1st Bde.*
B.-Gen.	B.-Gen.	B.-Gen.	B.-Gen.	B.-Gen.
Robertson	Jones	Grant	Pigott	Earl Percy
5th	18th 65th	3rd Bn. Arty.	38th	23rd
45th	49th	43rd	1st Bn. M.*	59th
63rd	2nd Bn. M.*	52nd	47th*	44th
35th	40th	22nd	10th	4th

Two squadrons of dragoons on each flank.

The order of battle of the Continental army six days later was as follows:

Commander-in-Chief
General George Washington

Major-General Lee		*Major-General Ward*
B.-Gen. Sullivan	B.-Gen. Green	B.-Gen. Spencer
1st N.H. (Stark)	1st R.I. (Varnum)	2nd Conn. (Spencer)
2nd N.H. (Poor)	2nd R.I. (Hitchcock)	6th Conn. (Parson)
3rd N.H. (Reed)	3rd R.I. (Church)	Mass. Bn. (Walker)
Mass. Bn. (Nixon)	Mass. Bn. (Gardner)	Mass. Bn. (Reed)
Mass. Bn. (Mansfield)	Mass. Bn. (Brewer)	Mass. Bn. (Learned)
Mass. Bn. (Doolittle)	Mass. Bn. (Little)	Independents

* Marines

3rd Conn. (Putnam)
Mass. Bn. (Glover)
Mass. Bn. (Frye)
Mass. Bn. (Bridge)
Mass. Bn. (Woodbridge)
Mass. Bn. (Sargent)

B.-Gen.
Thomas
Mass. Bn. (Ward)
Mass. Bn. (Thomas)
Mass. Bn. (Fellows)
Mass. Bn. (Cotton)
Mass. Bn. (Danielson)
Mass. Bn. (David
Brewer)

Canada, 1775-1776

On 16 June 1775 the so-called 'Separate army' was formed to secure the Canadian frontier. The Separate army officers were commissioned by Congress, and so it should be considered part of what was to become the Continental army. On 30 August the Americans under Schulyer and Montgomery advanced towards Montreal from Fort Ticonderoga, which had been seized from the British by Ethan Allen in May of the same year, with the intention of linking up with a force commanded by Colonel Benedict Arnold, consisting of some 1,300 volunteers taken from the New England regiments around Boston. A detachment of Montgomery's force captured Fort Chambly on 19 October, and on 2 November the British garrison of Fort St John, 500 strong, surrendered. Eleven days later Montgomery occupied Montreal without a struggle. Arnold, meanwhile, was heading towards Quebec along the Chaudière River, suffering such hardships that by the time he reached his objective he had lost half his force. Joining up with Montgomery they attacked Quebec on 31 December, and were repulsed with heavy casualties, including Montgomery who was killed.

In April 1776 the Americans planned to renew their offensive, but the vanguard of 10,000 British under Burgoyne sailed up the River St Lawrence, so the Americans abandoned the siege and retreated to Ticonderoga. The Separate army and the survivors of Arnold's volunteers combined to form what was henceforth known as the 'Northern army'.

1. Great Britain: Aide-de-camp to a General Officer

The earliest orders for the uniforms of staff officers in the British army which appeared in 1767 were extremely vague, but specified red coats with blue facings and silver embroidery. Some time after this date the design of the coat was altered to that shown here, which is based on paintings of the Siege of Gibraltar (1782). Aides-de-camp wore two gold epaulettes and had gold-laced button-holes spaced singly or 'regular'. By an order of 1778, brigade-majors were given similar uniforms but with silver epaulettes and lace.

2. Great Britain: Lieutenant-General the Hon Thomas Gage

The first regulation dress for field-marshals and general officers was introduced in orders published in

1767, which described a uniform coat, and a 'frock', or undress coat, and also gave the various rank distinctions. In 1772 the colour of the coat linings, waistcoats and breeches was changed from buff to white. In this portrait of Gage, based on the original at Firle, he wears the frock of a lieutenant-general, with its old-fashioned small standing collar, which has a blue patch at the front with a gold button and embroidered loop. Generals had their button-holes placed 'regular', and major-generals in pairs.

3. Great Britain: Adjutant-General

Adjutant- and quartermaster-generals wore silver epaulettes and laced button-holes set in threes. Deputies had their laced loops set on in pairs, and if attached to cavalry formations wore a single epaulette on the left, and if to infantry formations a single epaulette on the right. The crimson waist-sash had a false rosette in front and fastened at the back under the coat with tapes. The officer shown here wears stockings and shoes as would be normal when not riding or on the march. The celebrated and unfortunate Major André, as adjutant-general, would have worn just such a uniform.

4, 5, 6. United States: Provincial Alarm Companies and Minutemen

As the disputes with the mother country worsened the colonists began to arm the local militia and form special Alarm Companies of minutemen who could turn out, fully armed and equipped, at a moment's notice. Uniforms do not seem to have been in evidence either at Lexington and Concord or Bunker Hill where, according to Lieutenant Clarke of the marines, both officers and men wore their own clothes, nor did he see 'any colours to their regiments'. What little we know of the dress of the rebel militia suggests that they turned out in much the same way as they would for hunting or shooting and sporting pictures of the period have suggested the figures shown here.

Naturally with differing drills and weapons, the militia were no match for regular troops in close order but as they showed early on they were not to be despised as skirmishers. As Lord Percy said of them,

Whoever looks upon them merely as an irregular mob will find himself much mistaken; they have men amongst them who know what they are about, having been employed as Rangers against the Canadians and Indians – nor are their men devoid of the spirit of enthusiasm, as we experienced yesterday, for many of them concealed themselves in houses and advanced within ten yards to fire at me and the other officers, though they were morally certain of being put to death themselves in an instant . . .

7. Great Britain: Grenadier, 43rd Regiment

The dress of the regiments of the British army was modified in 1768 in accordance with a Royal Warrant which gave details of the various regimental distinctions. The right flank, or grenadier company, of the infantry battalion had long ceased to perform its original task, but was still composed of the biggest and tallest men of the regiment. The new fur grenadier caps introduced in 1768 had a japanned metal plate at the front bearing the King's Crest and the motto NEC ASPERA TERRENT. In some regiments it appears that the old cloth mitre caps were retained in use with the addition of a fur border. Grenadiers were further distinguished by the 'wings' on their shoulders, and the match case on the cartouche box belt. The grenadier shown here is dressed in accordance with the watercolours in the so-called MS 'Grenadier Book' of 1768 in the Prince Consort's Library, Aldershot, and would have appeared like this on the march to Concord. He wears his waist sword-belt over his shoulder for comfort's sake, and carries his knapsack in the middle of his back, with the straps over the shoulders in Indian fashion, as opposed to the earlier method, slung over one shoulder.

8. Great Britain: Officer, 23rd, or Royal Welch Fusiliers

Fusilier regiments were introduced into the British army in 1702 by the Duke of Marlborough, for the purpose of protecting the train of artillery. Although they no longer carried out this rôle, they still wore the appurtenances of grenadiers, although their caps were slightly lower. Officers were distinguished chiefly by their sashes and gorgets, but an embryo system of distinguishing ranks by means of epaulettes was just starting. Field officers and officers of grenadiers wore two epaulettes, and captains and subalterns one only on the right shoulder. The Prince of Wales's feathers on the epaulettes of the officer shown here were a regimental and not a rank badge. After their unfortunate experiences at Lexington and Concord, where they were deliberately picked off by the rebel marksmen, officers tried to dress more like their men and abandoned the half-pike, or espontoon, in favour of the fusil, or short musket, which necessitated the wearing of a cartouche box.

9. Great Britain: Sergeant, Grenadier Company, 18th or Royal Irish

The sergeant shown here has the plain white lace on his coat, and a crimson sash with a central stripe of the facing colour as specified in the 1768 Warrant. Like the officer in Fig. 8 he wears short gaiters or 'half-spatterdashes' which were popular for hunting and shooting, were adopted by the light infantry and soon copied by the whole army. He carries a musket and has a shoulder-belt for his bayonet.

10. United States: Militiaman

This version of the American militiaman, with his cap inscribed

'Liberty or Death' – a foretaste of the French revolution – is based on a British caricature of the times. He is armed with a tomahawk, besides his firearm, and carries his belongings wrapped in a blanket and worn as a bandolier.

11. United States: Officer of Militia

Since officers of the militia were elected by their companies, they were often little better than the men they tried to command, and generally differed little in appearance. The officer shown here, however, is quite smartly dressed in civilian clothes and wears a crimson sash round his waist as a sign of his officer status. He is armed with a small sword and half-pike although very often these were abandoned in favour of fusils or muskets.

12. United States: Private, 4th Connecticut Regiment of 1775 (Colonel Benjamin Hinman)

This regiment, one of six raised by the state of Connecticut, existed from 1 May to 20 December 1775. Each was to have ten companies of 100 privates with the usual complement of officers, N.C.O.s and drummers. On 14 June 1775 they were taken into Continental pay until December 1775 when most of the men returned home on the expiry of their enlistments. Two companies of this regiment were garrisoned at Fort Ticonderoga. The broad-brimmed hat, the jacket of nautical cut and the striped trousers all feature in deserter descriptions of the time.

13. Great Britain: Sergeant, Light Company, 5th Regiment

The distinctive dress of the light infantry company attached to each battalion of infantry in 1771 was developed during the fighting against the French in Canada during the Seven Years War, and afterwards it fell into disuse until its revival. The essential differences were the cap, of which there appears to have been a bewildering variety according to regiment, the red waistcoat, a leftover from the earlier period, and the half-gaiters, which were soon adopted by the whole army. In addition, the light infantry wore their pouches on a waist-belt, at the front, and carried powder horns and tomahawks as well as their bayonets. The cap shown here, of a distinct regimental pattern, is based on an example formerly in the Museum of the Royal United Services Institution.

14. Great Britain: Officer, Light Company, 4th, or King's Own

The painting of an officer of the 4th Regiment by Gainsborough, upon which this figure is based, was formerly thought to be of Captain the Hon John Rawdon, but it is now believed to be of Richard Bullock, who was lieutenant of the light company in 1779. The uniform of light company officers in the 4th seems to have undergone little modification, apart from the shortening of the coat, the wearing of half-gaiters, and the carrying of a fusil and bayonet and a curved sabre. The hat was probably worn as an alternative to a cap of some sort. The dark coloured band round the lower left arm is interesting and may be some form of field-sign to distinguish between the various battalions of light infantry which were formed by amalgamating the light companies of regiment. A similar dark armband appears in a portrait of Lieutenant Griffiths of the marines.

15. Great Britain: Officer, Light Company, 10th Regiment
This officer, based on a contemporary painting, wears a short coat, red waistcoat and black leather equipment. His cap, the details of which are not clear in the original, appears to be of black leather with a silver star badge on the front.

16. United States: Private, Pennsylvania Rifle Regiment
Raised in July 1775 from frontiersmen from the western borders of the Province to form a regiment of six companies, each of sixty-eight men, the Pennsylvania Rifle Regiment took part in the siege of Boston. Two companies accompanied Benedict Arnold to Canada and were captured at Quebec. During the winter of 1775–1776 it was reorganised as the 1st Continental Regiment. This figure wears typical Indian dress, in this case (as described in deserter advertisements), dyed black. The hat with a feather or tuft of animal's fur, the fringed rifle frock and the leggings complete an outfit which Washington would have liked to issue to all his army.

17. United States: Officer, 1st Rhode Island Regiment of 1775 (Varnum)
Under Christopher Greene, cousin of the celebrated Nathanial Greene, the 1st Battalion of this regiment made the heroic march with Arnold to Quebec. Captain Samuel Ward of the regiment is shown in Trumbull's painting of the death of Montgomery at Quebec. The figure here, based upon the painting, shows the type of winter clothing used in the Canadian forests. The pouch and belt are of 'wampum' or Indian beadwork. When the regiment was disbanded in December 1775 some of the men went into the new 9th or 11th Continental regiments.

18. United States: Private, Colonel Seth Warner's Battalion of Green Mountain Boys
The disputes between the settlers of the New Hampshire Grants and the New York Colonial officials caused the men of the various towns of New Hampshire and Vermont to form military companies, known as the 'Green Mountain Boys'. In June 1775 Congress formed them into a battalion of 500 men under Seth Warner. The battalion was badly cut up in the Canadian campaign and the survivors were formed into Warner's regiment which fought at Saratoga and like the two Canadian regiments was classed as a special unit separate from the Continental line. The figure here wears the normal uniform of the regiment with the addition of a wampum pouch and belt and a tomahawk.

19. Great Britain: Private, Grenadier Company of Marines

The grenadier companies of the two battalions of marines concentrated in Boston appear to have been formed after their arrival, and their special grenadier caps were sent out to them. They had a distinctive plate with an eight-pointed star with a fouled anchor in the centre, surmounted by a crown, within a laurel wreath above a scroll inscribed NEC ASPERA TERRENT. While it is known that light companies of marines also existed, no details of their dress have come down to us apart from a cap of doubtful authenticity.

20. Great Britain: Officer, Battalion Company of Marines

This figure represents a field officer, with his two epaulettes and riding boots, much as Major Pitcairn must have looked when he led the British advance guard at Lexington and was killed at Bunker Hill. He wears his sword from a shoulder-belt with a silver plate bearing the badge of the marines, the Royal Crest. When the army left Halifax for New York in 1776 the marines remained behind and took no more part in the main campaigns, although they were, of course, used in isolated actions.

21. Great Britain: Gunner, Royal Regiment of Artillery

At this time the Royal Regiment of Artillery was organised into battalions of companies consisting of a captain, a captain-lieutenant, first and second lieutenants, three lieu-tenant-fireworkers, three sergeants, three corporals, eight bombardiers, twenty gunners, sixty-two matrosses, and two drummers. The establishments varied but at the time of the American war the strengths seem to have been at their highest.

The gunner here wears his hair clubbed, and has white breeches, stockings and 'half-spatterdashes', as specified in orders. Apart from his bayonet-belt, he carries a pouch of white-red buff leather of a special artillery pattern, suspended from a belt with sockets in the front for a small hammer and two spikes for clearing the vents of artillery pieces; with this he wears a powder horn on a red cord. In his hand he holds a portfire for igniting the powder in the vent of the cannon.

22. United States: Private, 4th Independent Maryland State Troops

Seven companies, each of 100 men, were raised in January 1776 to join Washington in New York. The 4th Company was commanded by Captain Hindeman who with a budget of £3 10s per head clothed his men in dyed Osnaberg linen hunting shirts with red collars and cuffs. The state also raised two companies of matrosses and one of marines (see Fig. 150).

23. United States: Officer, Colonel Sargent's Massachusetts Battalion

On 19 May 1775, the state of Massachusetts raised twelve battalions of infantry each of 500 men in ten companies. These battalions were taken into Continental pay on 14 June 1775 and served until the following December. The green coats, and black facings of Colonel Sargent's battalion are mentioned in deserter descriptions. The yellow cockade in the hat denotes the rank of field officer.

24. United States: Colonel Patterson's Massachusetts Battalion Private

Another of the twelve battalions raised in May 1775, with a similar history to Colonel Sargent's battalion. The blue coats with buff facings are mentioned in deserter descriptions.

25. Great Britain: Sergeant, Battalion Company, 52nd Regiment

Battalion company sergeants normally carried halberds and swords, but, like the officers, they soon adopted fusils, bayonets, and cartouche boxes. Regiments with buff facings wore buff waistcoats and breeches, and often left their equipment un-pipeclayed. He has the usual plain white lace and a crimson sash with a stripe of the regimental facing colour. The canvas knapsacks were usually painted the same colour as the regimental facings, with the regiment's title, in gold, on a red ground.

26. Great Britain: Pioneer, 59th Regiment

In every infantry battalion a certain number of non-commissioned officers and men were appointed to act as Pioneers to carry out minor engineering tasks which might occur on the march or in action. Their equipment included special caps, leather aprons, saws, axes and so on.

27. Great Britain: Private, Battalion Company, 64th Regiment

This man wears the normal regimentals with the addition of long 'overalls' fastening at the ankle. These seem to have originated in Canada, and eventually became one of the most common garments of the war. He is on sentry duty protected from the weather by his blanket which is fastened round his neck with two tapes, as is shown in a figure in the 'Lennox' paintings of the 25th Regiment at Minorca. Overcoats, or 'Watchcoats' as they were called, were occasionally issued to sentries when available.

28. United States: Gunner, Lamb's New York Artillery Company

The American artillery at Bunker Hill did not distinguish itself, the rebels losing five out of their six field guns, and two of the five artillery companies retiring precipitately. Captain Lamb's company was raised in New York in July 1775 for Continental service. It took part in the Canadian campaign where it suffered severely. Alexander Hamilton, one of Washington's aides-de-camp, was an officer in this company (see Fig. 34). The blue and buff uniform was unusual for artillery units, the majority of whom wore blue, or black, faced with red. The canvas belt over the right shoulder has a drag rope for manhandling the guns attached to it.

29. United States: Officer, Colonel Knox's Artillery Regiment

Formed over the winter of 1775–1776 from the remnants of Colonel Gridley's regiment and other artillery units in Washington's army, this regiment consisted of twelve companies of five officers, three sergeants, three corporals, one drummer, one fifer, six gunners, six bombardiers, and thirty matrosses. At the end of 1776 most of the men returned to their homes. Colonel Knox was responsible for bringing the British pieces captured at Ticonderoga across country in the face of great difficulties, without which the siege of Boston could not have been pursued. Afterwards he commanded the artillery of the Continental army.

30. United States: Gunner, Rhode Island Train of Artillery

Captain John Crane's artillery company, one of the few well-trained and equipped militia units when the revolution broke out, joined the New England army before Boston in 1775. After May it appears to have been incorporated into Gridley's Massachusetts Artillery Regiment. An example of the distinctive caps worn by this regiment, belonging to Lieutenant Benjamin Carpenter, was picked up on the battle-field of Long Island, and is now in the Museum of the Fraunces Tavern, New York.

31. Great Britain: Corporal, Battalion Company, Marines

The marine corporal here wears a shoulder-belt for his bayonet with a brass oval regimental plate and half-spatterdashes. On his right shoulder he wears the white shoulder-cords which denoted a corporal.

Officers of marines were recommended always to dress their men at sea in 'sea-caps, jackets, and check shirts' and to take away and store their 'uniform coats, hats and caps ... also their white shirts, a pair of their stockings, and a pair of shoes . . .' By this means 'the marine officers will be qualified to turn out a clean, well-dressed guard for the reception of a superior officer; and when disembarked to do duty with land forces on shore, they will be able to make a soldier-like appearance ...'

Lieutenant MacIntire, writing in *A Military Treatise on the Discipline of the Marine Forces when at Sea, etc.*, 1762, lists the contents of the marine's knapsack as, 'four check shirts, one white shirt, four pairs of coloured and one pair of white stockings, a pair of shoes made of tanned leather, which will save the expense of black-ball and brushes, a pair of shoe soles, a pair of spatterdashes, a black leather stock, a set of uniform buckles, a hair cockade, a hat-tuft, combs, and a small bag of hair-powder, a hair band, needles, and thread'.

32. Great Britain: Officer, Battalion Company, 5th Regiment
The officer shown here is dressed in accordance with the regulations in force at the beginning of the war. His sash and gorget are signs of his officer rank, and he is armed with a sword and half-pike. He wears black gaiters which reach up above the knee.

33. Great Britain: Private, Battalion Company, 38th Regiment
The private shown here is also dressed in accordance with the regulations except that he has a shoulder-belt for his bayonet instead of a waist-belt. The 38th was one of the regiments which wore their lace formed into 'Bastion' loops.

Charleston, 1776

In January 1776 General Sir Henry Clinton, with the 28th regiment and seven companies of the 46th, arrived at Cape Fear from Boston, to help rally the loyalists of North Carolina and Virginia. Unable to wait any longer for expected reinforcements he commenced operations, but the loyalists had been defeated at the Battle of Moores Creek Bridge by the time Cornwallis arrived from England with the 15th, 37th, 54th, and 57th regiments (May 1776). On 28 June Clinton (with a force of 2,000) decided to attack Fort Moultrie on Sullivan's Island overlooking Charleston and was repulsed with the loss of one ship and 200 men. He rejoined Howe, Gage's successor, at New York where he had moved from Halifax in June.

New York, 1776

In June Howe moved his army of 32,000 from Staten Island and prepared to attack the Continental army commanded by Washington (20,300) in and around New York. On 17 August Howe with 20,000 men attacked Brooklyn Heights, on Long Island, defended by Israel Putnam with 7,000. Holding Putnam with two frontal assaults and attacking his left flank with the bulk of his force, Howe drove the Americans back to Manhattan with some 2,000 casualties against 377 British.

On 15 September the British landed at Kip's Bay and occupied Manhattan. The Americans fled up West side, halting at Harlem Heights where they stopped the British advance. Howe, therefore took the water route up the East River to New Rochelle, whereupon Washington retreated to White Plains and set up another defensive position, leaving Greene with 5,400 men to garrison Forts Washington and Lee, two strongpoints guarding the approaches to the Hudson River.

On 28 October Howe attacked Washington's force of 13,000 at White Plains, forcing him to withdraw to the north. Having split the Americans he turned south. Washington was worried by the possibility of a threat to

Fort Washington and of a British invasion of New Jersey, so he crossed the Hudson with 5,000 men and marched south, leaving Generals Lee and Heath with 8,000 men on the east side of the Hudson to hamper the British. Washington was too late, however, and on 16 November Howe overran Fort Washington and its garrison of 2,000 with 450 casualties. Immediately, Cornwallis with 5,000 men was sent across the Hudson to take Fort Lee, thus securing New York and clearing the Hudson for the British fleet. Washington was forced to retreat across New Jersey to the far side of the Delaware River.

On 26 December he made a sudden crossing of the Delaware and surprised 1,000 Hessians at Trenton. On 2 January 1777, Cornwallis with 6,000 advanced from New Brunswick towards Trenton, leaving men at Princeton and Maidenhead. Washington thereupon re-crossed the Delaware and on 3 January by-passed Cornwallis to attack Princeton. Cornwallis was left in the open, opposite Trenton, while Washington retired to his winter quarters at Morristown in the Jersey hills.

The British Order of Battle, August 1776

Commander-in-Chief
Sir William Howe

Lt.-Gen. Clinton
B.-Gen. Leslie

| 2nd Bn. | 3rd Bn. | 1st Bn. |
| Light Infantry | Light Infantry | Light Infantry |

B.-Gen. Cleveland

| 2nd Bde. | 3rd Bde. | 1st Bde. |
| Artillery | Artillery | Artillery |

First Line

M.-Gen. Pigott	*M.-Gen.* Agnew	*M.-Gen.* Smith	*M.-Gen.* Robertson	*M.-Gen.* Matthews
28th	44th	22nd	4th	2nd Bn. Gds.
49th	64th	54th	27th	
35th	57th	63rd	45th	1st Bn. Gds.
5th	23rd	43rd	15th	
2nd Bde.	*6th Bde.*	*5th Bde.*	*1st Bde.*	

Cavalry on the flanks

Second Line

Lt.-Gen. Earl Percy
B.-Gen. Erskine

M.-Gen.
Grant
40th
55th
46th
17th
4th Bde.

1st Bn. 71st
3rd Bn. 71st
2nd Bn. 71st

M.-Gen.
Jones
10th
38th
52nd
37th
3rd Bde.

Corps de Reserve

Lt.-Gen. Earl Cornwallis
M.-Gen. Vaughan

2nd Bn.
Grens.

4th Bn.
Grens.

3rd Bn.
Grens.

1st Bn.
Grens. 33rd

Hessian Division

Lt.-Gen. v. Heister

M.-Gen.
v. Mirbach
Lossberg
Rall
Knyphausen

M.-Gen.
v. Stirn
Erbprinz
Mirbach
Donop

Col.
v. Donop
Linsingen
Minegerode
Block

Col.
v. Lossberg
Trümbach
Ditfurth

The American Order of Battle, New York, 1776
M.-Gen. Israel Putnam

B.-Gen.
John Fellows
(Mass.)
Worcester Co. Militia (Holman)
Plymouth and Bristol Co. Militia (Cary)
Berkshire Co. Militia (Smith)
14th Cont. (Glover)

B.-Gen.
James Clinton
(Mass.)
13th Cont. (Read)
3rd Cont. (Learned)
23rd Cont. (Bailey)
26th Cont. (Baldwin)

B.-Gen.
John Morin Scott
(N.Y.)
1st Independent Bn. (Lasher)
2nd N.Y. Co. Bn. (Malcolm)
Militia (Drake)
Militia (Humphrey)

M.-Gen. William Heath

B.-Gen.
George Clinton
(N.Y.)

B.-Gen.
Thomas Mifflin

Militia (Nichol)
Militia (Thomas)
Militia (Swartout)
Militia (Palding)
Militia (Graham)

5th Pa. Bn. (Magaw)
3rd Pa. Bn. (Shee)
27th Cont. (Hutchinson) Mass.
16th Cont. (Sargent) Mass.

M.-Gen. Joseph Spencer

B.-Gen.
James Wadsworth
(Conn.)

B.-Gen.
Samuel Holden Parsons

Levies (Silliman)
Levies (Gay)
Levies (Sage)
Levies (Selden)
Levies (Douglas)
Levies (Chester)
Levies (Bradley)

17th Cont. (Huntington) Conn.
22nd Cont. (Wyllis) Conn.
20th Cont. (Durkee) Conn.
10th Cont. (Tyler) Conn.
21st Cont. (Ward) Mass.

M.-Gen. John Sullivan

B.-Gen.
Alexander McDougall
1st N.Y. Regt. (late McDougall's)
3rd N.Y. Regt.
19th Cont. (Webb) Conn.
Artificers (Brewer) Mass.

B.-Gen.
Stirling
Maryland Regt. (Smallwood)
Delaware Bn. (Haslett)
Pa. Rifle Regt. (Miles)
Pa. Musketeers (Atlee)
Pa. Militia (Lutz)
Pa. Militia (Kachlein)
Lancaster Co. Pa. Militia (Hay)

M.-Gen. Nathaniel Greene

B.-Gen.
Nathanial Heard
(N.I.)

B.-Gen.
John Nixon

New Levies (Forman)
Militia (Johnstone)
New Levies (Martin)
New Levies (Newcomb)
New Levies (Van Cortlandt)

1st Cont. (Hand) Pa.
9th Cont. (Varnum) R.I.
11th Cont. (Hitchcock) R.I.
Mass. Bn. (Late Nixon's)
Mass Bn. (Prescott)
12th Cont. (Little) Mass.

B.-Gen.
Oliver Wolcott
Conn.
Militia (Thompson)
Militia (Hinman)
Militia (Pettibone)
Militia (Cooke)
Militia (Talcott)
Militia (Chapman)
Militia (Baldwin)
Militia (Mead)
Militia (Lewis)
Militia (Pitkin)
Militia (Strong)
Militia (Newberry)

B.-Gen.
Nathanial Woodhull
Long Island
Suffolk Co. Militia (Smith)
Kings and Queens Co. Militia
(Temsen)

Col. Henry Knox
Artillery (Mass.)

34. United States: Aide-de-camp to a General Officer

In common with the practice in Europe, Washington organised the Continental army into divisions and brigades, commanded by major- and brigadier-generals, assisted by brigade-majors and aides-de-camp. The discipline of the New England army before Boston, however, suffered because there was difficulty in recognising superior officers, who had no regulation uniforms. In July 1775 all general officers, their aides and brigade-majors were ordered to wear ribbons of various colours across the breast, under the coat, like the ribbons of orders of chivalry. Aides-de-camp and brigade-majors were to wear a green ribbon. The figure here is based on a portrait of Captain Alexander Hamilton, who was one of Washington's principal aides.

He is shown in the uniform of Lamb's Artillery Company (see Fig. 28) in which he at one time served.

35. United States: Commander-in-Chief

By the order of July, 1775, the commander-in-chief of the Continental army was to be distinguished by a blue ribbon. This portrait of General Washington is based on that painted by Charles Wilson Peale for John Hancock in 1776. The blue and buff uniform which Washington customarily wore later became the regulation dress for the staff of the Continental army (see Figs. 164, 165, and 166). The choice of these colours had political undertones, as they were the 'uniform' of the Whig party in England; their Tory opponents adopted blue coats with red collars and cuffs.

36. United States: Brigadier-General

The generals of the Continental army were at first hardly distinguishable from their men. General Israel Putnam had on nothing but a sword-belt over his waistcoat, looking better fitted 'to lead a band of ditchers or sicklemen than musketeers'. The normally dapper General Anthony Wayne appeared dressed 'for a character of Macheath or Captain Gibbet in a dingy red coat with a rusty black cravat, and tarnished laced hat'. General officers were always being held up by their own sentries, until the order of July 1775, by which they were to wear pink ribbons. Soon after this order was altered to differentiate between brigadier- and major-generals who were given purple ribbons. The figure here is based on a popular print of Brigadier-General Benedict Arnold, published in 1776.

37. Great Britain: Sergeant, Battalion Company, 1st Regiment of Foot Guards

A 'Brigade' of foot guards, 1,000 strong, formed by selecting fifteen men from each of the sixty-four companies of the three regiments, was sent to America in 1776, where it was immediately formed into two battalions. An order of 12 March 1776, announced that:

His Majesty has been pleased to permit the officers of the detachment to make up an uniform with white lace like the privates of their respective regiments; the Sergeants to have their coats laced with white instead of gold . . .

Officers and sergeants were also ordered to lay aside their spontoons and halberds and to arm themselves with fusils. The sergeant shown here is dressed in accordance with these orders, with the plain crimson waist-sash as worn by sergeants of the foot guards, and white lace formed into bastion loops, placed regularly, as on the dress of the privates of the regiment. The cartouche boxes of the foot guards were distinctive in that they had two brass buckles to which the belt was attached.

38. Great Britain: Officer, Light Company, Coldstream Regiment of Foot Guards

This officer is in campaign dress, with the broad-brimmed hat soon adopted by many regiments in America. His jacket is a cut-down version of the 'frock' or undress coat with white lace instead of gold and no epaulettes. He retains his sash and gorget however. The belt over his left shoulder supports a cartouche box, and that over his right shoulder a bayonet for his fusil.

39. Great Britain: Private, Grenadier Company, 3rd Regiment of Foot Guards

Apart from the half-spatterdashes this was the normal peacetime dress of the grenadiers of the regiment. The plain white lace loops placed in threes denoted the 3rd Guards, while the Coldstream Guards had them in pairs. The cap plates and the buckles of the waist-belts, here shown worn over the shoulder, differed for each regiment. The cap plates were all-metal with the Royal Arms. Those of the 1st Regiment were black, the Coldstream red and the 3rd white. The 1st Regiment had plain waist-belt buckles, the Coldstream a pierced oblong with a CG in the centre, and the 3rd a buckle with ends representing two 3's reversed; all the buckles were made of brass.

40. United States: Rifleman, 1st Continental Regiment

On 1 January 1776, Washington reorganised the Continental army into twenty-seven regiments of infantry. The 1st 'Continental or Foot Regiment in the Service of the United Colonies', and the only one of the twenty-seven to come from Pennsylvania, was formed from Hand's Pennsylvania Rifle Regiment. The regiments seems to have continued to wear frontier dress, as shown in Fig. 16.

41. United States: Private, 12th Continental Regiment

No less than sixteen of the twenty-seven new Continental regiments of 1776 came from Massachusetts. The 12th, commanded by Colonel Moses Little, was one of the few regiments properly uniformed in brown with red facings. An order of 4 April 1776, states that,

Col. Hitchcock's and Col. Little's regiments are to turn out to-morrow morning to escort his Excellency into town, to parade at 8 o'clock,

both officers and men dressed in uniform, & those of the non-commissioned officers and soldiers that turn out to be washed both face & hands, clean, their beards shaved, their hair combed & powdered, & their arms cleaned . . .

42. United States: Sergeant, 6th Continental Regiment

The 6th Continental Regiment of 1776, also known as 'Whitcomb's Rangers' after Colonel Asa Whitcomb, was another Massachusetts regiment which formed part of the Northern army on Lake Champlain. Deserter descriptions of the regiment mention brown coats with red or white facings, and seamen's clothing. Lack of uniform in the Continental army made it difficult to differentiate between officers, N.C.O.s and men. Rank badges had to be adopted which were not only clearly visible, but easily made from materials that were to hand. By an order of July 1775, N.C.O.s were to be distinguished by epaulettes, or strips of cloth, sewed on the right shoulder, red for sergeants, and green for corporals.

43. Great Britain: Grenadier, 42nd, or Royal Highland Regiment

The independent companies raised in Scotland in 1725 were called the 'Black Watch', because their duties included the prevention of cattle-stealing and blackmail. In May 1740 the companies were incorporated into a regiment of foot, which in 1749, was numbered the

42nd. In 1759 it became a royal regiment and was given blue facings. The regiment wore a uniform based on highland dress consisting of a blue bonnet, red jacket and waistcoat, belted plaid of government or '42nd Sett', diced hose and brogue shoes. Their weapons were musket and bayonet, dirk and broadsword, although, according to an inspection report for May 1775, the swords were unpopular with the men who found them cumbersome and preferred bayonets. A figure in the 1768 Grenadier Book shows that the grenadiers of the regiment wore fur caps, and had a red line in their tartan.

44. Great Britain: Light Company Officer, 42nd or Royal Highland Regiment

This figure is based on a portrait of Lieutenant James Stewart, probably painted in America. As the war progressed the regiment 'disposed of their plaids etc . . . to purchase a more commodious dress for the American service'. Cartouche box, belt and half-spatterdashes, not shown in the original painting, have been added. A 'List of the officers of the Army serving in North America for 1783' (printed in New York) contains the following MS note against the 42nd:

> Scott. or Highland Dress formerly. At present the same as the British regiments of infantry that have short coats, except that they continue to wear the bonnet.

In Halifax in 1784, the men were wearing 'white strong ticken trousers with short black gaiters'.

45. Great Britain: Officer, 71st Highland Regiment (Fraser's Highlanders)

The first new regiment to be raised as a result of the American emergency was the 71st, formed in the latter part of 1775 by Simon Fraser, Master of Lovat, as a gesture of gratitude to George III for the return of his father's estates. During the Seven Years War he had raised a highland regiment, the 78th, which had been disbanded in 1763, and the new regiment contained many officers and men from the old 'Fraser's'. It was formed at Glasgow and served under Howe, Clinton and Cornwallis, the greater part of the regiment surrendering at Yorktown. It was disbanded in 1783. The officer here wears full highland dress with a broadsword in his hand; he also carries a highland pistol and a dirk.

46. United States: Private, 14th Continental Regiment

A provisional regiment of minutemen was raised in Marblehead, Massachusetts, on 14 May 1775 by a prominent ship owner, John Glover. Most of the men were seamen and fishermen and many of them retained their seagoing clothes when the regiment joined the Continental army. On 1 January 1776 the regiment became the 14th Continental Regiment. Descriptions of the dress of the regiment mention 'light coloured coats', drab or brown, with red facings. A well-disciplined regiment, Glover's Marbleheaders achieved immortal fame by being selected to ferry the army across the frozen Delaware River on Christmas Eve 1776, prior to Washington's surprise attack on Trenton.

47. United States: Officer, 8th Continental Regiment

Colonel Enoch Poor's 2nd New Hampshire Regiment, formed on 20 May 1775, entered the Continental service in June 1775 and became the 8th Continental Regiment in January 1776. It served with the Northern army until the end of 1776 when its term of service came to an end. Its successor regiment, commanded by Nathan Hale, was captured at Hubbarton, Vermont, on 7 July 1777 and two colours of the regiment were taken at Fort Anne in August of the same year (See flags Figs. 211 and 212). Although officers in the Continental army retained crimson sashes and in some cases gorgets typical of the British army, and were armed with spontoons and fusils, from July 1775 their ranks were distinguished by cockades in the hat. These were red or pink for field officers, yellow for captains (changed in 1776 to white or buff) and green for subalterns.

48. United States: Private, 18th Continental Regiment

Originally Colonel Phinney's regiment, one of the twelve Massachusetts battalions raised on 19 May 1775. Shortly after entering Boston on 20 March 1776 the 18th Continental were supplied with coats and jackets made of undyed cloth straight off the loom, apparently with buff facings. In July 1776 they were selected with three other regiments to reinforce the Northern army on Lake Champlain. When the regiment was disbanded at the end of 1776 many of the men transferred to the 12th Massachusetts Regiment.

49. Provincials: Private, King's Royal Regiment of New York

One of the most celebrated of the Provincial corps, this regiment was raised in June 1776 in the backcountry of New York by Sir John Johnson, son of Sir William Johnson, Indian Superintendent of the Five Nations. With his regiment and John Butler's Rangers (see Fig. 119), he swept down the Mohawk valley from Montreal turning the region into a smoking waste. They were originally supplied with an English shipment of green coats with various coloured facings. The regiment wore red with blue facings from 1778 onwards, until they were disbanded in 1784.

50. Provincials: Major Robert Rogers, Queen's Rangers

In July 1776, the celebrated Rangers leader in the French and Indian wars formed the King's (later Queen's) Rangers from the Loyalists of New York and Connecticut. Its strength was to be ten companies of infantry. The portrait here is based on an old engraving which shows Rogers in what is believed to be the first uniform of his corps. In 1777 Lieutenant-Colonel French took over command of the Queen's Rangers. He was succeeded by Major Wemyss, and when he was wounded at Germantown the command passed to John Groves Simcoe (see Figs. 179, 183–5).

51. Provincials: Loyal American Association

In the autumn of 1775 General Gage formed at least three small units from the loyalist refugees flocking into the town of Boston. They were not uniformed, and were distinguished by various 'field-signs'. The Royal North British Volunteers wore blue bonnets with the cross of St Andrew; the Loyal Irish Volunteers, a white cockade; and the Hon Timothy Ruggles's Loyal American Association, a white scarf on the left arm. These corps were all short-lived and were never properly uniformed.

52. United States: Private, 2nd New York Regiment, 1775

The state of New York raised four regiments for Continental service in 1775, all of which served with the Northern army. By August 1775 they were all supplied with uniform coats, and according to one witness had acquired 'the air of Regulars'. The 2nd Regiment commanded by Colonel Goose van Schaick wore brown coats faced with blue.

53. United States: Private, Light Company, 2nd Canadian Regiment

On 10 November 1775, Congress raised a Canadian battalion which was followed in January 1776 by a second battalion. This battalion was recruited 'at large' and was not allocated to any state line, so it was generally known as 'Congress's Own' or 'Hazen's Regiment' after its commander. The regiment was engaged in the retreat across New Jersey in the autumn of 1776, and maintained an exceptionally good record throughout the war in spite of having all foreigners in the army, with the exception of those in Armand's corps, sent to it in 1781. Hazen's Regiment is one of the few that are known to have had a light company as early as 1776. They wore special caps emblazoned with C.O.R., for 'Congress's Own Regiment', and the motto PRO ARIS ET FOCIS.

54. United States: Private, 3rd New York Regiment, 1775

The 3rd New York Regiment of 1775 had a similar history to the 2nd Regiment. Commanded by Colonel James Clinton, the regiment wore grey, faced with green.

55. Hesse-Cassel: Musketeer, Regiment v. Trümbach

This regiment, raised in 1701, arrived with the first Division of Hessians, on 12 August 1776, and served in Colonel v. Lossberg's Brigade of Lieutenant-General v. Heister's Division. It fought at Brooklyn, White Plains, Fort Washington, at Savannah, Guildford Courthouse and Yorktown, returning to Germany in December 1783. Musketeers, unlike fusiliers and grenadiers, wore hats with tassels and pom-poms in regimental colours. The coats of the Hessian troops were distinguished by having Prussian-style cuffs with two buttons and holes set vertically, and six buttons on the fronts of their coats set on in pairs. After their arrival in North America they were issued with one-piece overalls made of strong ticking, in brown, red or blue stripes, or of plain canvas.

56. Hesse-Cassel: Standard-bearer, Fusilier Regiment v. Ditfurth

This regiment, raised in 1702, served in v. Lossberg's Brigade, and was present at Brooklyn, White Plains, Fort Washington, Rhode Island 1777–1779, New York 1780 and the Carolinas 1780–1781. Fusilier regiments, (the tactical distinction was purely nominal), wore special caps which consisted of a leather skull reinforced with metal bands, and a plate similar to those on the grenadier caps, but lower. The officers wore hats. Standard-bearers in German regiments (*Gefreiten-corporal*) were chosen from those whose physique, character and background made them suitable to become officers. They carried N.C.O.s canes, wore buff leather gauntlets and an oilcloth flag case with brass cap around the waist or over the shoulder. Accord-

ing to one authority, early in the war, the lapels of this regiment were trimmed all round with white lace.

57. Hesse-Cassel: Grenadier, Musketeer Regiment Prinz Carl

This regiment, raised in 1702, arrived on 12 August 1776, fought at Brooklyn, White Plains and Fort Washington, and served at New York from 1777–1780. The grenadier companies of the musketeer and fusilier regiments, together with the Grenadier Regiment v. Rall and two companies of the Garde Regiment, were formed into four grenadier battalions of four companies each. The first three to arrive were brigaded together under Colonel v. Donop. The grenadier caps, of Prussian design, were made of coarse cloth, held in shape by three whalebone supports and sewn over with worsted tape. The front plate, from the same metal as the buttons, was 10 in. (25.4 cm) high by 9 in. (22.9 cm) at the base, and the bottom of the back part of the cap was metal. The whole was surmounted by a worsted tassel in regimental colours. Officers of grenadiers wore hats not caps.

58. United States: Private, Delaware Regiment (Haslet's)

Lefferts shows this regiment with leather caps, but recent research has now revealed that the example which he copied is almost certainly a modern reconstruction. In fact, instead of caps there is evidence that the regiment received 'felt hats' in 1776. The style of hat shown here is based on a representation 'of an American soldier' on the Grand Seal of Delaware State. The regiment served with distinction in 1776 and its commander John Haslet was killed at Princeton.

59. United States: Officer, 2nd New York Regiment

This regiment was one of four new battalions raised to serve with the Continental army for the year 1776. New York had raised four regiments in 1775 which had served with the Northern army. The four regiments of 1776 served with the main army. The 2nd New York Regiment was commanded by Lieutenant-Colonel Peter Gansevoort from August to November 1776, and the uniform shown in this figure is based on a coat and waistcoat reputed to have been worn by him.

60. United States: Private, Maryland Regiment (Smallwood's)

This regiment was formed in 1776 from independent companies in Baltimore and Annapolis, one of which, Mordecai Gist's Baltimore Independent Cadets, wore red coats with buff facings. When the regiment joined Washington's army at New York, however, the men were dressed in hunting shirts of various colours. After covering Washington's retreat at the Battle of Long Island, the remains of the regiment were formed during the winter of 1776–1777 into the 1st Maryland Regiment, which was virtually wiped out at the Battle of Camden.

61. Hesse-Cassel: Fusilier,Regiment Erbprinz

Raised in 1680, this regiment arrived at New York on 12 August 1776, and formed part of Major-General v. Stirn's Brigade. It fought at Brooklyn, White Plains, Fort Washington and was in New York from 1777–1780. It took part in the southern campaign with Arnold and Cornwallis and was captured at Yorktown in 1781. In 1780 the fusilier caps of the regiment were replaced by cocked hats and the rose facings were changed to crimson.

62. Hesse-Cassel: Sergeant, Musketeer Regiment v. Donop

Raised in 1687, this regiment was also part of Major-General v. Stirn's Brigade. It fought at Brooklyn, White Plains, Fort Washington and during the Pennsylvania campaign of 1777–1778. It was in New York from 1778–1780. Sergeants in the Hesse-Cassel infantry were distinguished by black and white hat pom-poms and tassels, sword knots and a row of gold or silver lace round their hats and cuffs. They normally carried canes and were armed with halberds and swords, but in America they tended to abandon these in favour of fusils and bayonets.

63. Hesse-Cassel: Drummer, Musketeer Regiment v. Mirbach

Raised in 1745, this regiment was part of Major-General v. Stirn's

Brigade, and fought at Brooklyn, White Plains and Fort Washington. It was one of the regiments taken by the Americans at Trenton, and the survivors served in Pennsylvania in 1777–1778 and in New York in 1778–1780. The drummers' coats and carriage-belts were laced in red and white, and they wore leather aprons. The hoops of the drums were painted in the Hessian colours and the brass shell was embossed with the lion of Hesse-Cassel.

64. United States: Private, 3rd New York Regiment of 1776

This regiment had a similar history to the 1st New York Regiment and served with the main army until it was disbanded at the end of the year. 'Blue or brown regimentals turned up with green' are mentioned for this regiment in deserter descriptions for 1776.

65. United States: Officer, 3rd Pennsylvania Battalion of 1776

This battalion raised early in 1776 was reorganised in the winter of 1776–1777 as the 4th Pennsylvania Regiment of 1777. It took part in the New York campaign and surrendered to General Knyphausen after the taking of Fort Washington. The orders regarding rank badges issued in 1775 specified green cockades for subaltern officers. The officer shown here also has a crimson sash, and is armed with a fusil and a bayonet which is suspended from a waist-belt worn over the shoulder. Brown faced with white is mentioned in several deserter descriptions for this regiment in Pennsylvania in the spring of 1776.

66. United States: Private, 1st Pennsylvania Battalion of 1777

This battalion was created in the winter of 1776–1777 from new recruits and Continental army veterans. 'A regimental brown coat faced with green the buttons marked Pa, Bn, button-holes bound with red', is mentioned in the *Maryland Journal* for 18 February 1777.

67. Hesse-Cassel: Corporal, Fusilier Regiment v. Lossberg

This and the following two regiments which arrived at New York in August 1776 formed Mirbach's Brigade, and were surprised at Trenton at the end of December 1776. Over 700 prisoners were taken from the three regiments, and the survivors were formed into one battalion under Rall, known as the 'Combined Battalion'. As the captives were exchanged, the regiments were reformed and resumed their separate identities. The Regiment v. Lossberg was raised in 1672. It fought at Brooklyn, White Plains and Fort Washington, and reappears in the states for the New York garrison after being reformed from new drafts. From the autumn of 1779 part of the regiment was in Canada and part in New York. In January 1781 a composite unit of detachments from Lossberg and Knyphausen, 234 strong, appears on the states. Corporals in the Hesse-Cassel service were distinguished by a band of white lace round the top of the cuffs.

68. Hesse-Cassel: Officer, Musketeer Regiment v. Knyphausen

Raised in 1684, this regiment fought at Brooklyn, White Plains and Fort Washington. It reappears in the New York states for November 1778, and from 1779–1780 was in Canada. Hessian officers were chiefly recognisable by their gorgets, which bore the arms of Hesse-Cassel in enamel, and their red and silver sashes. Their hats were edged with gold or silver lace and had a black cockade with gold or silver button and loop. Originally armed with half-pikes and small-swords, they soon gave these up in favour of fusils and bayonets as shown here.

69. Hesse-Cassel: Private, Grenadier Regiment v. Rall

This regiment was raised in 1760 and fought at Brooklyn, White Plains and Fort Washington. It was in Pennsylvania in 1777–1778 and it returned to New York in August 1778; then, as Wallworth's it was ordered to Savannah in November 1778, and was in Georgia from January 1779 to June 1780. In September 1780 it was with Cornwallis in South Carolina and was still there in September 1781. The grenadier here wears a fur pack of the Prussian model and a linen haversack. He wears his waist-belt over his shoulder.

70. United States: Corporal, 6th Virginia Regiment of 1777

Early in 1777, the 6th Virginia was reorganised and served until 14 September 1778, when it was incorporated into the 2nd Virginia Regiment. A deserter of Captain Fox's company of the regiment disappeared, according to the *Pennsylvania Packet* for 13 May 1778, in a 'Light gray coat and waistcoat, the coat faced with green osnabrug overalls, a small round hat with a piece of bearskin in it'. This description has formed the basis for this figure, who in addition has the green shoulder-strap on the right shoulder denoting a corporal.

71. United States: Private, 9th Pennsylvania Regiment of 1776

Raised in October 1776 as part of an expanded quota from Pennsylvania, this regiment served until January 1781 when it was disbanded on Washington's orders, after the mutiny of the Pennsylvania Line. Deserter descriptions for the regiment in Pennsylvania during the spring of 1777 mention new brown uniform coats, turned up with red, and in one case a light infantry cap is mentioned.

72. United States: Sergeant, 7th Pennsylvania Regiment of 1777

In the winter of 1776–1777, the former 6th Pennsylvania Battalion was reformed as the 7th Pennsylvania Regiment. Under this title it served until January 1781. The regimentals of the corps appear to have been blue with red facings. The red shoulder-strap denotes a sergeant.

73. Hesse-Cassel: Private, Garrison Regiment v. Huyn

Among the regiments of the second division of Hessians which arrived at New York in October 1776, there were several reserve or garrison regiments. They had originally been clothed in blue waistcoats and breeches, but before leaving these were changed for straw-coloured garments. Regiment v. Huyn was raised in 1760 and fought at Fort Washington. It was at Rhode Island from 1777–1779, in Charleston in January 1780 and in South Carolina until September 1781.

74. Hesse-Cassel: Sergeant, Musketeer Regiment Wutginau

Raised in 1688, this regiment fought at Fort Washington. It was at Rhode Island from 1777–1779, and in New York from 1779–1780. The garrison regiments wore single-breasted coats with two rows of buttons and false worked button-holes.

75. Hesse-Cassel: Pioneer, Garrison Regiment v. Stein

This regiment was raised in 1760 and fought at Fort Washington. It was in New York from 1777–1778 and in Halifax from November 1778–1781. Pioneers wore leather aprons and caps rather than hats and carried axes and saws.

76. United States: Private, Colonel William R. Lee's Additional Continental Regiment

In January 1777 sixteen additional regiments were raised for service with the Continental army. This regiment was formed by William R. Lee mainly from Massachusetts recruits. In April 1779 it was amalgamated with Colonel Jackson's Additional Continental Regiment. According to the *Continental Journal* for 19 December 1777, some of the men wore brown regimental coats faced with red and felt hats.

77. United States: Private, Colonel Henley's Additional Continental Regiment

Formed in January 1777 by David Henley from Massachusetts recruits, this regiment was amalgamated with Colonel Jackson's Additional Continental Regiment in April 1779. The *Independent Chronicle* for 5 March 1778 mentions a deserter wearing a red coat faced with light blue, and a light infantry cap.

78. United States: Corporal, Colonel Hartley's Additional Continental Regiment

Formed in January 1777 by Thomas Hartley from Pennsylvania and Maryland recruits. In January 1779 it formed part of the new 11th Pennsylvania Regiment. The *Pennsylvania Gazette* for May 1777 mentions a blue regimental coat with white facings.

79. Anspach-Bayreuth: Gunner, Artillery Company

This company arrived at New York in 1777 and served in the Pennsylvania campaign of 1777–1778. They were attached to the two Anspach-Bayreuth infantry regiments throughout the war (see Fig. 86).

80. Hesse-Cassel: Private, Jäger Company

A first detachment of jägers arrived at New York on 12 August 1776 with General v. Heister's division, and a second with v. Knyphausen in the following October. For the rest of the war they took part in nearly every skirmish and battle. First raised in 1758 from trained huntsmen, the jägers were considered as an élite corps. The green uniform dates back to the formation of the Prussian Field Jäger Corps in 1744, although huntsmen and foresters had worn green clothing long before that. In the 1770s their rifles, often the personal property of the jägers, were outmoded and inferior to those carried by their American counterparts. Officers wore gold shoulder-cords and the sergeants' coats were edged with gold lace. The waist cartridge pouches bore the crown and cipher CFCA in yellow metal. The Anspach-Bayreuth jägers wore similar uniforms with green waistcoats and buff leather breeches.

81. Hesse-Cassel: Gunner, Artillery Company

The three artillery companies sent to America represented the entire artillery corps of Hesse-Cassel, and in fact two of them had to be specially raised and trained. After their arrival at Long Island in 1776, they took part in virtually every important engagement of the war, including Brooklyn, White Plains, Fort Washington, New York and Rhode Island 1777–1778, the Carolinas 1780, Virginia 1781 and South Carolina 1781. Each company consisted of five officers, fourteen N.C.O.s, three drummers and 129 gunners. Their guns appear to have been mainly light 4-pounders. There is no evidence, as Lefferts states, that Hessian bombardiers wore fusilier caps like the Prussians who had not worn them in action for some time before and had in fact abolished them for the artillery in 1750.

82. United States: Private, Colonel Samuel B. Webb's Additional Continental Regiment

Raised in January 1777 by Samuel B. Webb from Connecticut recruits, this regiment was extremely well-disciplined, trained and dressed. It was always uniformed and even had a band. It was taken into the Connecticut line as the 5th Regiment on 18 July, 1780. Between 1778 and 1780 there are several references to the red coats with yellow facings worn by this regiment.

83. United States: Officer, Colonel Sherburne's Additional Continental Regiment

This was raised in January 1777 by Henry Sherburne from Connecticut and Maryland recruits. On 1 May

1780 it was broken up and many of the men went into Colonel Webb's regiment. Early in 1779, there are several references to deserters in brown coats faced with yellow.

84. United States: Private, Colonel Spencer's Additional Continental Regiment

Oliver Spencer raised this unit in January 1777 from New Jersey recruits. From 1777 to mid-1778 it was sometimes referred to as the 5th New Jersey Regiment. It was disbanded in January 1781. The *Pennsylvania Packet* for 22 April 1777 refers to a deserter in a 'blue coat with red facings, blanket trousers buttoned down his legs'.

85. Anhalt-Zerbst: Private, Infantry Regiment

This regiment, 625 strong, arrived at Quebec on 12 September 1778, where by an administrative muddle the men were kept aboard their transports for no less than three months. Thereafter they remained on garrison duty until the end of the war. A second contingent, which arrived at New York in August 1781, wore a curious hussar-type uniform with a cylindrical felt shako, Hungarian boots and a red cloak.

86. Anspach-Bayreuth: Grenadier Sergeant, 2nd Brandenburg-Anspach Infantry Regiment

The two Anspach-Bayreuth infantry regiments with their attendant artillery arrived at New York in June 1777, and remained brigaded together throughout the war. They served at Philadelphia 1777–1778, New York 1778, Rhode Island 1779 and New York October 1779–May 1781, after which they went to Virginia. They were taken at Yorktown, and remained in captivity until May 1783, when they were exchanged. The 1st Regiment, which had similar services, wore blue coats with red collars, cuffs and lapels. The battalion men of both regiments wore hats bound with white lace.

87. Waldeck: Private, 3rd Infantry Regiment

Raised specially for British service by the recall of mercenaries from Holland, and by the merciless conscription of the citizens of Waldeck, the regiment arrived at New Rochelle on 23 October 1776. It served in the New York campaign (Fort Washington) and remained there until November 1778, when it went to Pensacola. In West Florida in January 1780, it was captured by the Spaniards at Mobile in February of the same year. It was exchanged in 1781 and served in the New York area until 15 July 1783, when it returned home. The regiment consisted of a grenadier company of 134 officers and men, and four musketeer companies of 130 officers and men each. The regiment was accompanied by two 3-pounder field guns manned by two bombardiers and twelve gunners. The grenadiers wore bearskin caps after the Dutch fashion without plates, together with yellow cloth bags trimmed in white lace and finished with a white tassel.

88. United States: Sergeant, 1st Continental Light Dragoons

The American Corps of Light Dragoons dated from the autumn of 1777 when Brigadier-General Count Casimir Pulaski was appointed 'Commander of the Horse' with four weak regiments serving under him. The 1st Light Dragoons, as Bland's Virginia Horse, reported to Washington in the winter of 1776 at Morristown, and were mustered in Continental service on 31 March 1777. In December 1776 two uniforms seem to have been in use, one blue faced with red and one brown faced with green. Orders issued by Bland in the spring of 1777 give one of the most complete descriptions known of a Continental regiment even to the extent of specifying a comprehensive system of rank markings. Field officers were to have two fringed epaulettes, captains one on the right shoulder, and a gold strap on the left shoulder, and staff officers two plain gold straps. Quartermaster-sergeants had green shoulder-straps, edged with yellow braid and with a green rosette on the right side, sergeants had green shoulder-straps with a green rosette and yellow fringe on the right side, and corporals green shoulder-straps, with a green fringe on the left side. The trumpeters of the regiment wore green faced with brown. The American light dragoons, while performing good service throughout the war, never achieved great strength, and in 1780 the 1st was amalgamated with the 3rd Light Dragoons. This combined force served in the Yorktown campaign with the 'Light Corps' and with Lauzun's legion at Gloucester Point where they were opposed to Simcoe's and Tarleton's legions.

89. United States: Officer, 3rd Continental Light Dragoons

Raised in January 1777 by George Baylor from Virginians, Pennsylvanians and Marylanders. On 27 September 1778, the regiment was ambushed at Tappan, New York, only twenty escaped out of 104, Baylor being wounded and captured. In 1780 it suffered further losses in the Carolinas, and after Camden was combined with the 1st and 4th regiments to form four troops, which served at Cowpens and Guildford Courthouse. The combined unit was designated the 3rd Legionary Corps in 1781. Portraits of Captain Roger Nelson, and of Colonel William Washington who commanded the regiment after Baylor's capture, together with an engraving by Chodowiecki published in Germany, provide evidence for the white uniform with light blue facings worn by this figure.

90. Great Britain: Dragoon, 16th, or the Queen's Own Light Dragoons

One of the two regular light dragoon regiments serving in North America, the 16th, or Burgoyne's, received the title of the

Queen's Own in 1766, and changed their facings from black to blue. While in America the regiment had a troop of twenty-nine dismounted dragoons, equipped with loose mantles carried over their knapsacks, and brown cloth gaiters instead of boots. In place of their swords they carried hatchets and wore leather caps like the light infantry. When the 16th left America the effective men and horses were drafted to the 17th Light Dragoons. The trumpeters of the 16th wore red coats faced with blue and yellow lace with a blue stripe. Their hats were edged with red feathering and they carried both trumpets and bugle horns.

91. Great Britain: Officer, 17th Light Dragoons

A small party of this regiment was present at Bunker Hill, and the bulk of the regiment fought at Long Island, White Plains, Newport Rhode Island, Germantown, Philadelphia and Monmouth, Forts Clinton, Montgomery and Pound-ridge. A detachment was attached to Tarleton's legion, and while in the south, wore white sheepskin turbans round their helmets in place of the red shown here. The housings of the regiment, not shown here, were white, edged with lace with a black centre stripe, with XVII L.D. on the housings and holster caps. Officers had silver tassels on the corners of both housings and holsters. The farriers of both regiments wore blue with cuffs and collars of the facing colour, laced like the dragoons, and adopted small black bearskin caps, like the infantry pioneers, with a white metal horseshoe on a black metal plate. They had leather aprons and an axe carried on a shoulder-belt. Some carried saws or spades under the right arm on a belt like a carbine-belt. In place of holsters they had churns for their tools. Their housings were blue with black bearskin flounces, decorated with a white horseshoe on the forepart and a white hammer and pincer on the hindpart.

Canada, 1776–1777

After the failure of Arnold's proposed attack on Canada in 1776, the Americans hastily assembled a flotilla of fifteen vessels which lay waiting for the British in the shelter of Valcour Island on Lake Champlain. On 11 October the British with twenty-five vessels passed the island before seeing the Americans, and were forced to beat up to windward in order to attack. The two fleets exchanged fire for five hours, often at close quarters, and the Americans lost two vessels and suffered severe damage to others. At nightfall the British anchored in line across the channel, assuming that they had trapped their quarry, but the Americans slipped away during the night, and next morning were ten miles away. In the ensuing chase Arnold lost two leaking vessels and beached and burned six others, and he and his men made their way through the forests to Crown Point. The Americans lost ten vessels and eighty men and the British one vessel and forty men.

Saratoga, 1777

In June Colonel St Leger with 1,600 British and Indians started a diversionary advance down the St Lawrence to Oswego which he hoped to reach by the Mohawk valley. At the same time Burgoyne with 7,500 started his advance south towards Albany. On 6 July 2,300 Americans evacuated Fort Ticonderoga and retreated to Fort Edward at the junction of the Mohawk and the Hudson. The pursuing British, exhausted from the rough terrain and suffering from supply problems, were forced to halt on the bank of the Hudson opposite Saratoga. On 16 August a British and Brunswick raiding party sent out to obtain supplies was badly defeated at Bennington.

Meanwhile on 3 August St Leger had laid siege to Fort Schulyer. 1,600 Americans under Herkimer and Arnold rushed to its relief, but Herkimer was ambushed and stopped in a battle which was so costly to St Leger that when Arnold approached he was forced to retire to Oswego and Montreal, leaving Burgoyne to fend for himself. Burgoyne, his position untenable because of lack of supplies and reinforcements, crossed the Hudson and, in two battles at Freeman's Farm and Bemis Heights, he was defeated by an American force of 17,000 men. On 17 October he surrendered his force of 5,700 to the Americans, at Saratoga, who, in contravention of the terms of the surrender, imprisoned them.

British Order of Battle for Burgoyne's Expedition
Advanced Guard (Fraser)
Grenadiers, Light Infantry, 24th.
1st Brigade (Phillips)
9th, 47th, 53rd.
(The 47th were left to guard
the boats, the 53rd were left
at Ticonderoga, and the 9th were
added to the 2nd Brigade.)
2nd Brigade (Hamilton)
20th, 21st, 62nd.
v. Riedesel's Brigade
Brunswickers.
(Prince Friedrich Regiment left
at Ticonderoga.)
King's Royal Regiment of New York (Johnson's)
Butler's Rangers
Indians

Pennsylvania, 1777

In the summer of 1777, Howe found his land route to Philadelphia blocked by Washington and embarked his force, sailing up the Chesapeake, until, on 11 September, he defeated Sullivan at Brandywine Creek. The Americans, who suffered 1,000 casualties retired to Chester, and on 26 September Howe entered Philadelphia, which had been hastily abandoned by the Continental Congress.

On 3 October Sullivan met another reverse at Germantown, where the gallant British defence of Chew House enabled reinforcements to reach them from Philadelphia.

On 19 December Washington withdrew his depleted forces to Valley Forge while Howe with 19,000 passed the winter in quarters around Philadelphia.

British Order of Battle in the Pennsylvania Campaign
Major-General Hon. Sir William Howe, KB

Artillery
Detachments from several companies
of the 4th and 5th Battalions, Royal
Artillery, under Lt.-Col. Samuel
Cleveland.

General Knyphausen's Column
One Squadron, 16th Light Dragoons
1st Brigade (Major-General Vaughan)
4th, 5th, 23rd, 49th
2nd Brigade (Major-General Grant)
10th, 27th, 28th, 40th
Major-General Stirn
Linsing, Lengkerke, Leib, Mirbach
71st Highlanders, Three battalions
Queen's Rangers

General Cornwallis's column
Two squadrons, 16th Light Dragoons
Mounted and dismounted chasseurs
3rd Brigade (Major-General Grey)
15th, 33rd, 44th, 55th
4th Brigade (Major-General Agnew)
17th, 37th, 46th, 64th

Foot Guards, two battalions
Light Infantry, two battalions

Grenadiers, two battalions
Hessian Grenadiers, three battalions
Ferguson's Corps of Riflemen

(Hesse-Cassel and Anspach jägers
divided between both columns)

Valley Forge

On 19 December 1777, Washington's army, reduced to some 11,000 men, crossed the Schuykill River and reached the windswept, heavily wooded hills of Valley Forge, where they set about building themselves an entrenched camp to the plans of a young French engineer, Louis du Portail. Clad in rags and ravaged by starvation and sickness, only 5,000 men were fit for duty by February. At this point the newly arrived Baron v. Steuben, who had served in the Prussian army was appointed drill master by Washington. Starting with a single squad, by hard work and perseverance he gradually built up a disciplined army. When Washington appointed General Nathanial Greene to be quartermaster-general, the health and appearance of the men improved correspondingly, and when spring came Washington could march out of Valley Forge at the head of a completely reformed army.

Troops wintering at Valley Forge 1777–1778

B.-Gen. *William Woodford*		B.-Gen. *Charles Scott*	
7th Va.	(McClanachan)	8th Va.	(Bowman)
11th Va.	(Daniel Morgan)	12th Va.	(Wood)
			(Grayson)

B.-Gen. *Anthony Wayne*		*2nd Pennsylvania Brigade*	
1st Pa.	(Chambers)	4th Pa.	(Cadwalader)
2nd Pa.	(Bicker)	5th Pa.	(Johnston)
7th Pa.	(Irwin)	8th Pa.	(Broadhead)
10th Pa.	(Nagel)	11th Pa.	(Humpton)

B.-Gen. *Enoch Poor*		B.-Gen. *John Glover*	
3rd N.H.	(Scammell)	4th Mass.	(Shepard)
1st N.H.	(Cilley)	1st Mass.	(Vose)
2nd N.H.	(Hale)	13th Mass.	(Wigglesworth)
2nd N.Y.	(Van Cortland)	15th Mass.	(Rigelow)
4th N.Y.	(Livingston)		

B.-Gen.
Ebenezer Learned
2nd Mass.	(Bailey)
9th Mass.	(Wesson)
8th Mass.	(Jackson)

B.-Gen.
George Weedon
2nd Va.	(Febiger)
4th Va.	(Read)
10th Va.	(Green)
3rd Va.	(Marshall)
14th Va.	(Lewis)

B.-Gen.
William Maxwell
1st N.J.	(Ogden)
2nd N.J.	(Shreve)
3rd N.J.	(Dayton)
4th N.J.	(Martin)

B.-Gen.
Jedediah Huntington
5th Conn.	(Bradley)
2nd Conn.	(Webb)
7th Conn.	(Swift)

B.-Gen.
Lachlan McIntosh

1st N.C.	(Clark)
2nd N.C.	(Patten)
4th N.C.	(Polk)
3rd N.C.	(Sumner)
5th N.C.	(Buncombe)
6th N.C.	(Lamb)
8th N.C.	(Armstrong)
7th N.C.	(Hogun)
9th N.C.	(Williams)

B.-Gen.
John Paterson
10th Mass.	(Marshall)
14th Mass.	(Bradford)
11th Mass.	(Tupper)
12th Mass.	(Brewer)

B.-Gen.
Peter Muhlenberg
1st Va.	(Hendricks)
5th Va.	(Parker)
9th Va.	(Matthews)
6th Va.	(Gibson)
13th Va.	(Russell)
German Regt.	(Weltner)

B.-Gen.
Thomas Conway
3rd Pa.	(Craig)
6th Pa.	(Magaw)
9th Pa.	(Butler)
12th Pa.	(Cooke)
Cont.	(Malcolm)
Cont.	(Spencer)

B.-Gen.
James M. Varnum
1st R.I.	(Greene)
2nd R.I.	(Angell)
8th Conn.	(Chandeler)
4th Conn.	(Durkee)

B.-Gen.
Henry Knox
Artillery Brigade
1st Cont. Art.	(Harrison)
2nd Cont. Art.	(Lamb)
3rd Cont. Art.	(Crane)
4th Cont. Art.	(Proctor)

Unattached

| Cont. | (Henley) |
| Cont. | (Jackson) |

Most of the four regiments of light dragoons, parts of the two regiments of artillery artificers and some of the engineers, sappers and miners were also at Valley Forge.

In May 1778 Howe returned to England and was succeeded by Clinton who decided to evacuate Philadelphia while peace negotiations took place. On 17 June he crossed the Delaware and disembarked his force of 19,000 for their march to Brunswick and the Raritan River. On 28 June Cornwallis was attacked at Monmouth Court House (or Freehold), by Lee and Lafayette. Lee tried to entice the British by retiring but his movement degenerated into a retreat for which he was relieved of his command by Washington.

On 5 July 1778, the British regained New York in safety, having narrowly escaped the French fleet under d'Éstaing which arrived off the capes of Delaware on 8 July.

92. United States: Private, 13th Virginia Regiment

Raised in October 1777 as part of Virginia's increased quota, this regiment was in Brigadier-General Peter Muhlenberg's brigade at Valley Forge. The *Pennsylvania Gazette* for 22 April 1778 mentions a blue coat with yellow facings for this regiment. Baron v. Steuben noted that at Valley Forge he saw officers whose full uniform at the grand parade consisted of either dressing-gowns or suits made out of blanketing. Officers were permitted to go out to dinner in any clothing they could muster, while the rank and file, going on leave, might spend a day or two making up suits out of blankets so as to be decently clad on their journey home.

93. United States: Sergeant, 1st Battalion Philadelphia Associators

The Associators of Philadelphia were companies of volunteer militia of which only two are known to have been active in 1775. Within a few weeks of Lexington, however, these had been increased to four uniformed battalions and several independent companies. In late 1776, or early 1777, they were re-organised as the Philadelphia Brigade under Brigadier-General Cadwalader, and eventually became the 3rd Pennsylvania Brigade. The uniform of the Associators was brown with different coloured cockades and facings for each battalion.

94. United States: Private, Light Infantry, 1st Battalion Philadelphia Associators

The light infantry companies attached to the battalions of Associators appear to have been dressed in green with 'smart caps and feathers'.

95. Great Britain: Bugler, 2nd Battalion, Light Infantry

We are fortunate in having some very valuable information about the dress of the British army during the Pennsylvania campaign of

1777–1778, obtained from two *gouache* drawings made by the Italian artist Xavier Gatta, probably to the instructions of a British officer who was present. The first shows the defence of the Chew House at Germantown which so held up the American advance. Some of the figures represent light infantrymen, and as the 2nd Battalion was involved in this action we may assume that they come from this battalion. They wear slouch hats with black tufts, red waistcoats, black equipment and white overalls, a very practical dress, and a considerable change in appearance from the early days of the war.

96. Great Britain: An Officer of Light Infantry
This conjectural figure of an officer of a regiment with green facings is based partly on contemporary paintings by Wheatley, and partly on the Gatta drawings mentioned above. Short single-breasted jackets with collars and pointed cuffs became very popular during the second part of the war, particularly for cavalry units, both British and American.

97. Great Britain: Private, Battalion Company, 40th Regiment
The men of the 40th Regiment, defending the Chew House in Gatta's drawing, differ from the light infantry by having white equipment and half-gaiters instead of overalls. One would, however, have expected their breeches and equipment to have been buff, as this was the colour of the regiment's facings. The officers were dressed like the men but had a red and a white feather in their hats.

98. United States: Corporal, 4th Connecticut Regiment of 1777
This regiment was organised early in 1777 and served until January 1781. While at Valley Forge under Colonel John Durkee, those men who were lucky enough to receive uniforms were provided with 'short brown coats . . . double breasted, without lapels, but with red collars and cuffs . . .'

99. United States: Private, Hall's Delaware Regiment
After Haslet's death at Princeton in December 1776 (see Fig. 58), Colonel David Hall and a cadre of Haslet's former officers reformed the regiment for the 1777 campaign. It continued to give good service until it was virtually wiped out at the Battle of Camden. One of the best-dressed and equipped regiments in the army, the men reportedly wore blue coats faced with red, and hats bound with yellow lace. In the southern campaign they were issued with shoes, hunting shirts and blue and white striped overalls. The figure here carries one of the japanned tin boxes for ammunition which were improvised to overcome the shortage of leather cartouche boxes.

100. United States: Private, 1st Connecticut Regiment of 1777
Organised in early 1777, commanded by Jedediah Huntington,

this regiment served until the reorganisation of the Connecticut line in 1781, when most of the men went into the 5th Connecticut Regiment. The *Connecticut Gazette* between 1777 and 1779 carried numerous reports of red coats, with either white or blue facings, for this regiment.

101. Great Britain: Grenadier, 21st, or Royal North British Fusiliers

The regiments shown in this and the next two figures took part in Burgoyne's ill-fated expedition. For this campaign, according to Lieutenant Thomas Anbury, writing in April, 1777.

> ... the commanding officers of the different regiments have received orders to reduce the men's coats into jackets, and their hats into caps, as it will be the means of repairing their present clothing, and be more convenient for wood service, that when the army takes the field, they will in a manner, be all light infantry. The regiments have the hair that is attached to their caps of different colours ...

The figure here, while having his jacket shortened, retains his fur grenadier cap. These were reported as new in 1774. Fusiliers were to have black bearskin caps, made like the grenadiers, 'but not so high; and not to have the Grenade on the Back Part'.

102. Great Britain: Officer, Light Company, 53rd Regiment

An inspection report on the 53rd in June 1769 mentions gold embroidered button-holes for the officers. The short coat or jacket shown here has elaborate wings and pointed cuffs with two buttons and loops.

103. Great Britain: Drummer, 34th Regiment

Drummers and Fifers of line infantry regiments wore coats of the facing colour, except for royal regiments who wore red, faced and lapelled in blue, and regiments with red facings who wore white coats, faced and lapelled in red. These coats were to be laced 'in such Manner as the Colonel shall think fit'. The drums were to be of wood; the front part of the wooden shell was to be 'painted with the Colour of the Facing of the Regiment with the King's Cypher and Crown and the Number of the Regiment under it'. The drummers' and fifers' caps were to be of black bearskin with an insignia on the front, 'the King's Crest, of Silver plated Metal, on a Black Ground, with Trophies of Colours and Drums.' The number of the regiment appeared on the back, 'as also the Badge, if entitled to any, as ordered for the Grenadiers'. They were to have short swords with a 'Scimetar Blade'.

104. United States: Lieutenant, 3rd Massachusetts Regiment

This regiment was raised in November 1776 and served until

November 1783. The uniform of a Lieutenant Leonard Chapin, stolen from his house according to the *New York Packet* of 21 October 1779, consisted of 'A blue lapelled coat edged with red, Continental buttons, . . . resembling silver, a good silver epaulet, lined with red; the said coat had been turned, and was lined with blue'.

105. United States: Lieutenant, 8th Massachusetts Regiment

This regiment served from November 1776 to June 1783. A deserting officer, noted in the *Boston Gazette* for 20 December 1777, wore a 'Pale blue uniform coat, faced with red, and a gold epaulet on his right shoulder'.

106. United States: Sergeant, 14th Massachusetts Regiment

This regiment served from January 1777 to January 1781. The *Independent Chronicle* for 22 October 1778 reported a deserter wearing a 'dark brown regimental coat, faced with light blue, reddish-brown waistcoat, peach blossom trousers'. Blue coats faced with white are also mentioned.

107. Great Britain: Private, Battalion Company, 9th Regiment

The following three figures represent regiments that served with Burgoyne. This figure is based on a watercolour drawing of a battalion man of the 25th Regiment in Minorca during 1771, which shows some interesting non-regulation variations on the normal dress of the infantry. In the first place he wears his cocked hat back to front. In the second, his coat has been shortened and has no lace; moreover the cuffs have a different arrangement of buttons to the regulation coat. Third, he wears a waistcoat with the edges piped in red.

108. Great Britain: Ensign, 24th Regiment

To judge from Graham's painting of the burial of General Fraser at Saratoga, the officers on Burgoyne's expedition were wearing their normal dress. The officer of the 24th Regiment shown here however has had his coat shortened. He carries the First, or King's Colour, of the regiment.

109. Great Britain: Sergeant, Battalion Company, 47th Regiment

On the evidence of Anburey's remarks quoted above, this battalion company sergeant wears the cropped hat and short coat usually associated with light infantry. He has the plain white lace and crimson sash with a white stripe which denote his rank.

110. United States: Private, 1st Maryland Regiment of 1777

This regiment was formed during the winter of 1776–1777 from a cadre of Smallwood's Maryland Regiment, and suffered severely at the Battle of Camden. Deserters described in the *Maryland Journal* for 9 December 1777 wore blue regimental coats faced with red. One wore a light infantry cap 'with silver lace round the edge, and B.L.I. in cypher in front'. This B.L.I. is thought to have stood for the Baltimore Light Infantry.

111. United States: Sergeant, 2nd Maryland Regiment of 1777

Formed in December 1776 from the remnants of several Maryland State Independent Companies, this regiment was decimated at Camden. Three deserters from the regiment are recorded in the spring and summer of 1777 as wearing blue coats faced with scarlet.

112. United States: Corporal, 6th Maryland Regiment of 1777

This regiment was created in December 1776, as part of the Maryland quota, and was virtually destroyed at Camden. Brigadier-General Smallwood formed the remains of the regiments at Camden into an effective regiment in the autumn of 1780, which was divided into two battalions in 1781. Several deserters are recorded in the late summer of 1777 as wearing brown or grey coats turned up with green.

113. Great Britain: Gunner, Royal Artillery

The following three figures represent units serving with Burgoyne. A set of drawings in the New York Public Library, attributed to F. v. Germann, shows a man of the Royal Artillery as reproduced here, suggesting that the artillery detachments with Burgoyne had cropped their hats and coats like the infantry.

114. Great Britain. Private, Light Company, 62nd Regiment

This figure is based on the v. Germann drawing of a battalion man of this regiment, with the usual alterations for the light company.

115. Great Britain: British sentry in winter clothing

This figure is based on the v. Germann drawing of a *British sentry in Canadian winter clothing*. There are many descriptions of this special winter clothing issued to the troops in America. It consisted of long blue cloth overalls 'such are worn by sailors', a cap, a pair of mittens, a 'capacious under-jacket, the sleeves being made of strong white corduory', and a Canadian overcoat, or *capot*, made of white melton, lined with sheepskin.

116. United States: Private, 2nd New Hampshire Regiment

Created, with the 1st New Hampshire Regiment, in the winter of 1776, this regiment served until March 1782, when the New Hampshire line was reorganised. According to Lefferts one company at least wore light blue coats faced with red and lined with white.

117. United States: Private, 3rd New Jersey Regiment

Recruited in the winter of 1776–1777, this regiment served until broken up in January 1781. According to Lefferts, the coats of the regiment were blue with red facings, and the hats were bound with white or yellow lace, although some leather caps were also worn.

118. United States: Sergeant, 5th New York Regiment

Raised in the summer of 1776, this regiment served in the Northern Department. In October 1777 most of the regiment was captured at Fort Montgomery. A deserter of the regiment, advertised in the *New York Journal* of 14 July 1777, wore a brown coat faced with blue. Another had a blue coat with button-holes bound with pale blue lace.

119. Provincials: Private, Butler's Rangers

Major John Butler, an officer of Sir William Johnson's Indian Department, was authorised to raise a corps of eight companies in September 1776. Two of the companies were to be recruited from persons 'speaking the Indian language and acquainted with their customs and manner of making war'. The Rangers, either as a body or in detachment, were used principally in frontier raids, usually in company with Johnson's, King's Royal Regiment of New York, and Brant's Mohawks. Two additional companies were raised in 1781, and the corps was not disbanded until June 1784. The intention was to arm the corps with rifles but as

each man bought his own, a variety of arms was used. The coats of the regiment were green with red facings, no doubt part of the original stock sent out from England.

120. Provincials: Loyalist Officer at the Burial of General Fraser

Graham's painting of the burial of General Fraser contains some interesting uniform details. One of the figures, standing in the right foreground and dressed as shown here with the addition of a hat and an Indian belt, appears to be an officer of a Provincial corps. Another officer, probably British, has a short red jacket with dark facings and brown Indian leggings.

121. Provincials: Private, Royal Highland Emigrants

This regiment of two battalions, which was taken on the regular establishment in the spring of 1779 as the 84th Regiment, was raised in the autmn of 1775 by Colonel Allan Maclean from the families of men of the 42nd, 77th and 78th Highlanders, who had settled in Canada at the end of the Seven Years War. Recruits were also obtained from Scottish emigrants in New York and North Carolina. The 1st Battalion served in Canada, and the 2nd in the Carolinas and Virginia. One detachment of the latter was at Yorktown, while another fought with Lord Rawdon in South Carolina. The regiment was disbanded in 1784. The uniform, facings and tartan of the 84th were the same as the 42nd, and one of the v. Germann drawings shows the plaid still in use.

122. United States: Private, Pennsylvania State Regiment, 1777

The so-called 'State Troops', as opposed to those of the 'State Line', were those who were neither in Continental service, nor militia. Early in 1777, apart from those in Continental service, Pennsylvania had a State artillery regiment, which was taken into Continental service in July 1777, and an infantry regiment, which was taken into Continental service in November of the same year. Three Pennsylvania newspapers around the date of 20 August 1777 report four deserters 'all dressed in blue, turned up with red, and white pewter buttons with the letters P.S.R. marked on them'.

123. United States: Private, 5th Pennsylvania Regiment, 1777

The 5th Pennsylvania Regiment was formed in January 1777 around a nucleus of Anthony Wayne's 4th regiment. Shortly afterwards Wayne was promoted, and later commanded a brigade at Yorktown. The 5th was one of the two regiments (the 9th was the other) which did not immediately join in the mutiny of the Pennsylvania line in 1781. The 5th retained their original blue coats with white facings until 1778 when the supply of white cloth ran out and red was used instead. From documents

relating to the 2nd Pennsylvania Regiment it appears that in some cases whole regiments, and not just the light companies, wore caps. The curious red flannel leggings are mentioned in connection with Wayne's Brigade in early 1779.

124. United States: Private, 11th Pennsylvania Regiment, 1777

The 11th Regiment was formed in October 1776 and served until its merger with the 10th Regiment in July 1778. The *Pennsylvania Evening Post* of 22 April 1777 mentions a 'new suit of regimentals, consisting of a light infantry cap, blue coat with scarlet cape and cuffs, white woollen waistcoat, new buckskin breeches'.

125. Brunswick: Dragoon, Regiment Prinz Ludwig

This regiment arrived at Quebec in June 1776, dressed and equipped for mounted service, but without horses and saddlery. Thus accoutred they took part in Burgoyne's expedition, and on 16 August 1777 were nearly all killed or captured in the raid on Bennington, Vermont, in an attempt to secure pack animals for Burgoyne and mounts for themselves. Their horizon blue uniforms, eminently unsuitable for forest fighting, were copied from those of the Prussian dragoons. Some authorities maintain that they kept their heavy jacked boots, but the v. Germann drawings show a man of the regiment in long infantry gaiters, which seems more probable. They were armed with carbines and heavy broadswords. The drummers of the regiment wore yellow, lined and faced with horizon blue, and trimmed with 'mixed lace.'

126. Brunswick: Officer, Jäger Company

This company arrived at Quebec in September 1776. It took part in the actions at Ticonderoga, Hubbardton, Freeman's Farm, Bemis Heights and Saratoga and was attached to v. Barner's Light Infantry Battalion (see Fig. 127). It was an élite corps of selected rangers and marksmen, mainly composed of the sons of German State Forest Rangers, and all ranks were armed with rifles and straight hunting swords. Their two musicians, presumably horn players, wore silver laced wings and cuffs, and their coats were trimmed with white, black and yellow mixed lace.

127. Brunswick: Sergeant, Light Infantry Battalion v. Barner

The four companies of light infantry, formed in 1776 and commanded by Major Ferdinand v. Barner, arrived at Quebec in June 1776 and fought at Ticonderoga, Hubbardton, Freeman's Farm, Bemis Heights and Saratoga. The battalion was formed of picked men, and their uniforms were of a better quality than the normal Brunswick clothing. All ranks like the jägers were armed with German rifles and hunting swords. Their musicians wore yellow coats with red linings and black facings, trimmed with white, black and yellow mixed lace.

128. United States: Private, 2nd Virginia Regiment, 1777

The 2nd Virginia Regiment was reorganised early in 1777, and there are several references in the *Virginia Gazette*, in the following September, to 'Regimentals of blue with white worsted binding'. From September 1778 to January 1783, during which time the regiment was captured at the taking of Charleston in May 1780, it was commanded by the former Danish officer Christian Ferbiger, under whom it became a model regiment.

129. United States: Officer, 2nd Rhode Island State Regiment, 1777

In 1777 the two regiments of State troops formed for the defence of Rhode Island were taken into Continental pay. They were employed guarding some 400 miles of coastline against British raiders. Colonel William Barton of the 2nd Regiment, whose portrait is shown here, distinguished himself by seizing the British commander at Newport, General Prescott, in his bed and removing him to the mainland in his nightshirt, without the loss of a single man.

130. United States: Private, Virginia State Line, 1778

In October 1778, twelve regiments of the Virginia line and the 1st and 2nd State Regiments, encamped at Elizabethtown, New Jersey, were issued with French-made coats of blue faced with red, red waistcoats, and blue, red or green breeches. By May 1779, however, v. Steuben found that the clothing of the 2nd Regiment was 'very bad', although their arms and accoutrements were in good order.

131. Brunswick: Sergeant, Infantry Regiment v. Rhetz

Raised in 1748, and reorganised as a two-battalion regiment in 1770, the Regiment v. Rhetz arrived at Quebec in September 1776, and fought at Ticonderoga, Hubbardton, Bennington, Freeman's Farm, Bemis Heights and Saratoga. On their arrival in North America the German regiments were wearing knee-high black cloth gaiters, but were soon issued with 'over-alls' made out of salvaged British tenting and sails, or from surplus naval stores of blue, red or white 'ticken', as worn by British sailors. The musicians of this regiment wore yellow coats lined in red, with white facings and silver lace.

132. Brunswick: Officer, Infantry Regiment v. Specht

Raised in 1714, and formerly known as the 2nd Battalion of v. Rhetz, this regiment arrived at Quebec in September 1776, and had a similar record to the Regiment v. Rhetz. Brunswick officers were distinguished by the cockades and elaborate silver lace on their hats, their gorgets, and their silver and yellow sashes and sword- and cane-knots. The musicians of the regiment wore yellow coats, lined and faced in red, trimmed with lace.

133. Brunswick: Private, Light Infantry, Infantry Regiment v. Riedesel

This regiment, formerly the 2nd Battalion of the Regiment Prinz Friederich, was raised in 1683, and arrived at Quebec in June 1776, and fought in the main engagements. Some of the German regiments that went to North America had their own light companies, who wore special caps. That shown here is decorated with the white horse of lower Saxony, and a feather in the Brunswick colour. It should be noted that the Brunswick infantry coats differed from the Hesse-Cassel coats in that they had only four buttons on the lapels, and had 'Swedish cuffs' with two buttons. The musicians wore yellow coats, lined red, with light blue lapels, and yellow and white mixed lace.

134. United States: 'American Officer', 1778

This figure, after a drawing by v. Germann, shows an officer of an unidentified Continental regiment in 1778. On 1 January 1778 Washington ordered 'New Cloathing' for the Continental army, which he described in a letter as 'a garment of the pattern of the Sailor's sea Jacket' which '... sets close to the body and by buttoning over the breast, adds much to the warmth of the Soldier'.

There could, he added, be 'a small cape and cuff of a different colour to distinguish the Corps'.

135. United States: Officer, 5th Virginia Regiment, 1777

The 5th Virginia Regiment was re-organised early in 1777 and commanded by Josiah Parker from April 1777 to July 1778. A miniature of Colonel Parker by Charles Willson Peale, part of the National Collection of Fine Arts, Washington, D.C., shows him in a typical Virginian uniform of blue, faced in red, with the addition of narrow gold lace on the button-holes.

136. United States: 'American Soldier', 1778

Another v. Germann drawing shows a private of an unidentified American regiment, with the unusual combination of a grey jacket with yellow facings.

137. Brunswick: Grenadier, Infantry Regiment Prinz Friedrich

Raised in 1683, this regiment was reorganised as a two-battalion regiment in 1770 and given the above title. It arrived at Quebec in June 1776, and, except for the grenadier company, remained at Ticonderoga and so escaped the disaster at Saratoga. The grenadier company, and those of the other Brunswick regiments, formed the grenadier battalion under Lieutenant-Colonel v. Breymann, which fought at Ticonderoga, Hubbardton, Bennington, Freeman's Farm, Bemis Heights and Saratoga. The musicians of the regiment wore yellow coats with red linings and light blue lapels, trimmed with yellow and white mixed lace.

138. Hesse-Hanau: Grenadier Sergeant, Infantry Regiment Erbprinz

This regiment arrived at Quebec in June 1776 and was brigaded with the Brunswick Regiment Prinz Friedrich, under its own commander, Brigadier-General v. Gall. It fought at Ticonderoga, Freeman's Farm, Bemis Heights and Saratoga. The appointments and clothing of this regiment were far more elaborate than those of the Brunswick army. The officers' sashes and sword-knots were in the Hesse-Hanau colours of silver, red and blue, and their hats had silver scolloped lace around the edge, and black cockades. The hats of the battalion companies had white scolloped lace and black cockades.

139. Hesse-Hanau: Gunner, Artillery Company

This company arrived at Quebec in June 1776 and fought in the same engagements as the Regiment Erbprinz. It also helped to man the guns of the British flotilla at the Battle of Valcour Island. Gun crews at this time usually consisted of a sergeant, a corporal who aimed the gun, two gunners to tend the vent, and to fire, and from six to twelve mattrosses, who had their own positions and duties. The higher numbered men usually man-handled the piece, by means of drag ropes and *bricoles*. The special pouch-belt carried pickers for cleaning the vent, and a powder flask with a brass plate bearing the arms of Hesse-Hanau. Among the Hesse-Hanau guns were four cast in France, which were captured at Quebec by the British in 1759, mounted on British carriages, and were eventually captured by the Americans at Bennington.

140. United States: Soldier in Canadian Winter clothing, 1778
This figure is based on v. Germann's drawing titled '*Ein Canadischer Bauer*', which shows the typical winter dress of the inhabitants of Canada, which was adopted by the participants on both sides.

141. United States: Officer, Continental Regiment of Artillery Artificers
In January 1777, Benjamin Flower, Commissary of Military Stores, raised several units of 'artificers' which fulfilled the rôle of the modern Ordnance Corps, supervising the manufacture and maintenance of weapons and transport. This drawing is based on a portrait of Flower attributed to James Peale, brother of Charles Willson Peale.

142. United States: Officer, Morgan's Rifle Corps, 1777
In the summer of 1777 Washington formed a corps of 500 riflemen, selected from the Main army, which he placed under the command of Colonel Daniel Morgan. The corps joined the Northern army in September 1777, and served with distinction in the Saratoga campaign. After rejoining the Main army in the winter of 1777–1778 the Corps was disbanded. This portrait of Morgan wearing a rifle frock and overalls, with an officer's sash and sword, is based on the figure in Trumbull's painting of the surrender of Burgoyne at Saratoga.

Raids and Counter-Raids

After Saratoga and the return of the British to New York from Pennsylvania, the war settled down to a deadlock. The British sat secure at New York and Rhode Island, while the Americans watched them in equal security from West Point and the Hudson Highlands. Throughout 1778, however, the backcountry of New York was torn by raid and counter-raid. In the spring Butler and Thyandanagea (alias Joseph Brant) swept through Wyoming and upper New York in a series of raids, which brought down Washington's wrath on the Six Nations of the Iroquois. In August General Sullivan led an expedition into the Iroquois country which resulted in their destruction as a great military power. Meanwhile, the strongly royalist Governor Tryon of New York led a series of raids against the seaport towns harbouring rebel privateers. In July 1779, Washington retaliated by taking Stony Point at the point of the bayonet, and the post of Paulus Hook, on the shore of the river Hudson opposite Manhattan.

Rhode Island

On 17 June 1778, war broke out between Britain and France, and on 11 July Admiral Comte d'Éstaing arrived off Sandy Hook, blockading New York for a short time. He then sailed to Narragansett Bay, where he made contact with General Sullivan to discuss operations against Rhode Island. In August Admiral Howe's fleet, based at New York, tried to bring d'Éstaing to battle off Newport, but both fleets were dispersed by a storm. D'Éstaing abandoned Sullivan, who had to abandon the Newport operations, and returned to Boston to effect repairs. He remained there until November when he left for the West Indies. Admiral Howe, after following d'Éstaing to Boston, gave up his command to Admiral Arbuthnot.

143. Iroquois: Red jacket

Red Jacket (1751?–1830) was a celebrated orator and chief of the Seneca, one of the Six Nations of the Iroquois, and one of those who supported the British in the American revolution. The Iroquois dress of the period was usually made of red or blue traders' broad-cloth, decorated with beads and quills. In this drawing, based on a print slightly later than the revolution, Red Jacket wears a blue cloth hunting shirt, red cloth leggings and deerskin moccasins. He wears a British officers' gorget and crimson sash, and is armed with a musket.

144. Iroquois: Joseph Brant (Thyandanega)

Perhaps the most celebrated of all Indian chiefs of the late eighteenth and early nineteenth centuries, Joseph Brant, a Mohawk, was supposed to have been the brother of Sir William Johnson's Indian wife. In any case he was brought up by Sir William, and educated at the school of one Dr Wheelock. Afterwards he was employed as an under-secretary at Johnson Hall. After deciding to throw in his lot with the British, Joseph Brant, along with Sir John Johnson and John Butler, was a prominent leader of the raids that ravaged the New York backcountry. After the war Brant led his people to Canada where they settled along the banks of the Great River, in what is now Ontario. He has been described as combining 'great personal activity and a fine manly figure, a good common education, undoubted bravery, and an intimate acquaintance with the manners and customs of civilisation ...' with ' ... all the subtlety, subterfuge, art, and, when he grasped the tomahawk in active war, all the cruelty of the forest savage'.

145. Iroquois: A Warrior

Until they were supplied with firearms, the Iroquois were mainly armed with the war club, the tomahawk, the bow, and occasionally with a short lance and a shield. As well as these weapons every brave carried a scalping knife. In the early colonial period vigorous attempts were made to prevent the Indians obtaining firearms, but by various means, both legal and illegal, they managed to acquire them. The firearm soon became an object of status, and Indians were prepared to pay vast sums for a weapon, whether it was in firing order or not; the price was often calculated on the basis of a pile of beaver skins as high as the length of the gun to be purchased. Muskets were generally reserved for raiding, or for hunting in time of famine.

The War at Sea

From the moment he took over the Continental army before Boston, Washington was conscious of the tremendous importance of sea-power. He had appealed for naval forces to run the British blockade, to attack ships bringing supplies to the British and to transport his own men and supplies. Congress, however, was extremely dilatory, and so Washington formed his own 'fleet' of six schooners and a brigantine, under the command of the Marblehead fisherman John Manley, with which he proceeded to harry the Royal Navy.

In the autumn of 1775, the Marine Committee of Congress voted to fit out five warships, and it was these, together with three other vessels, which formed the squadron of Commodore Esek Hopkins, which sailed for the Bahamas in February 1776. After attacking New Providence, where his squadron captured the governor, 100 cannon and two British frigates, he returned to Providence, Rhode Island. Unfortunately he had to land 100 sailors with smallpox, so that he was unable to man his vessels to escape the British invasion and was bottled up in Newport. In June one of the ships of his squadron, the *Andrew Dorea*, took two British transports carrying men of the 42nd Regiment, and in August John Paul Jones in the *Providence* raided Nova Scotia, returning to Newport in October with sixteen valuable prizes.

On 19 March 1776, Congress authorised the practice of privateering, and during that year some 143 vessels went to sea. By 1777, however, they had been almost halved by the Royal Navy. Privateering persisted and, during the course of the war, was responsible for the loss of sixteen British warships and nearly 3,000 merchantmen, bringing in a total haul of fifty million dollars.

Throughout 1777 the strength of the Royal Navy dominated the eastern seaboard of North America, and the embryo Continental navy, for which thirteen frigates were now building, was blockaded. With the desperate shortage of war material, blockade running became a vital task for American seamen, particularly to and from the Dutch colony of St Eustatius in the West Indies, where military stores bought by Congress were imported by European vessels as 'civilian goods'.

From the American point of view, the situation was saved by the entry of France into the war in 1778. The arrival of d'Éstaing off New York and his subsequent attempt to attack Newport have already been described. But elsewhere the Americans were taking the offensive, though on a small scale. John Paul Jones in the *Ranger* terrorised British shipping as near home as the Irish Sea, and in April he even landed in Britain, seizing the residence of the Earl of Selkirk. Sailing over to Ireland on 24 April, he met up with H.M.S. *Drake*, fought her and took her into Brest as a prize. He continued his actions into 1779 when, in the converted Indiaman *Bonhomme Richard*, he fought a remarkable action with the British frigate *Serapis*, which he again took into Brest as a prize, after his own ship had sunk.

1779 saw Admiral Byron pursuing d'Éstaing's fleet around the West Indies. Byron captured St Vincent on 16 June and Grenada on 4 July, but in an action off Grenada on 6 July, he was severely handled by the French admiral, who immediately sailed for Savannah. After the French and Americans failed to capture the town, he continued to France. The American cause suffered another defeat in July 1779, when the largest sea-going force ever assembled by the rebels, consisting of seven Continental warships, twelve privateers and twenty-two transports carrying 3,000 troops sailed to Penobscot on the Maine coast. After laying there for two weeks they were caught by the British and trapped wholesale in the Penobscot River. The American fleet was burned and 500 men were taken prisoner.

Between March and August 1780, Rodney, who was now in command in the West Indies, had three indecisive actions with the French and Spaniards under De Guichen. When the latter left for France in August, Rodney took half his fleet to New York in time to foil a projected descent on the city. In December he returned to the West Indies and in February 1781 seized the Dutch islands of St Eustatius and St Martin. He then sailed for England leaving Sir Samuel Hood in command.

On 22 March 1781, De Grasse left Brest for the West Indies with a large fleet and convoy. After inconclusive operations against Hood, he received in August a request for naval aid from Washington and Rochambeau. Collecting 3,000 available troops, he sailed north. He arrived in the Chesapeake on 30 August two days after Hood had looked in vain for him there, and had sailed on to New York to put himself under the command of Admiral Graves. The British fleet returned to the Chesapeake and on 5–9 September De Grasse with twenty-four ships sailed out to meet Graves with nineteen. After five days of fruitless manoeuvres Graves returned to New York leaving Cornwallis to his fate at Yorktown. The French squadron of eight ships at Newport, Rhode Island, under Barras now arrived off the Capes with siege artillery for Rochambeau.

After Yorktown, the Americans continued to privateer, but gradually the British regained the mastery of the sea with such victories as the Battle of the Saints fought on 12 April 1782. The revival of British sea-power, however, came too late to affect the outcome of the revolution.

146. United States: Midshipman, Continental Navy

While it may be safely assumed that the officers of the Continental navy dressed very much as they pleased, on 5 September 1776 the Marine Committee of Congress nevertheless issued the first dress regulations for the United States navy. These provided for a blue coat, with a standing collar, red lapels and cuffs, flat yellow metal buttons, a red waistcoat and blue breeches, as the basic dress. Captains had gold lace on their waistcoats and cuff flaps, while those of lieutenants were plain. Midshipmen had pale blue lapels to their coats. The midshipman here, as was the practice in the Royal Navy, wears a short jacket, a round hat and trousers.

147. United States: Captain Abraham Whipple, Continental Navy

Abraham Whipple of Providence, Rhode Island, who was reputed to have fired the first shot of the revolution at sea, took part in the 1772 incident when a royal revenue cutter, the *Gaspée*, ran aground off Narragansett and was burned by the local citizenry. Later he became a noted frigate captain in the Continental navy. In the expedition to Bermuda he commanded the sloop *Columbus*. Hs career ended when he surrendered the whole of his squadron to Admiral Arbuthnot at Charleston in 1780. With the exception of the cuff flaps, Whipple's dress in this portrait is remarkably like the regulations. In March 1777 a meeting of senior officers proposed a new uniform consisting of a blue coat, lined in white and laced with gold, with gold epaulettes, which was worn by some officers but never officially recognised. In February 1781 Congress issued an order which expressly forbade officers to wear 'any gold lace, embroidery or vellum, other than such as Congress or the Commander-in-chief of the Army or Navy shall direct . . .'

148. United States: Seaman, Continental Navy

There were no regulations for the dress of the seamen in the Continental navy, and their appearance was much the same as the sailors of the Royal Navy. The sailor here wears a round hat, short jacket and striped trousers, and is armed with a brace of pistols tucked into his belt.

149. United States: Private, Pennsylvania State Marines

150. United States: Officer, Maryland State Marines

In addition to the Continental, or 'Regular', marines, there were also marines in the navies maintained by several of the states.

151. Private: Continental Marines, 1776

The first recruiting centre for the Continental marines was the Tun Tavern in Philadelphia, the landlord of which, Captain Mullen, was commissioned in the marines in June 1776. Although he apparently never served at sea, he and his company saw action in the Trenton-Princeton campaign. In September 1776 the Marine Committee of Congress approved a green coat, faced in white, with a silver epaulette on the right shoulder for officers of marines. Probably because of the shortage of white material already noted in Pennsylvania (the depot of the marines remained at Philadelphia), the facings were changed to red in 1779. The marines were disbanded at the end of the war and were not reformed until 1798.

152. Great Britain: Captain (Three years' seniority), Royal Navy, Full Dress

A 'Uniform Military Cloathing' for the officers of the Royal Navy of blue with white facings, was first authorised in 1748. However, the 'Sea Commission Officers' who requested it at first showed little inclination to wear it. From 1767 to 1774 captains had one all-purpose uniform which after that date they were ordered to alter into a Full Dress which was to be worn with a white waistcoat and breeches. At the same time, however, they were given a blue 'frock' with blue facings and gold laced button-holes as an undress; senior captains wore

their buttons set in threes, junior captains in pairs and commanders regular.

153. Great Britain: Flag officer, Royal Navy, Undress

Flag-officers were officially restricted to one all-purpose uniform until 1783, but about 1774 they started wearing, as an undress, a uniform for which no authority has yet been found. This had white facings with gold laced buttonholes placed regular for all grades. The figure here, is based on portraits of Vice-Admiral Richard, Earl Howe, brother of the military commander-in-chief.

154. Great Britain: Lieutenant, Royal Navy

Lieutenants, who had complained about the plainness of their original uniform, were given white cuffs and lapels in 1768. At the same time they were ordered to wear white breeches and waistcoats.

155. Great Britain: Seaman, Royal Navy

It was more than 100 years after the introduction of a uniform for naval officers that seamen were given one. The formation of the Navy 'Slop' Office ('slops' being the sailors' traditional wide canvas trousers) in 1756 regularised the placing of orders to supply the dockyard stores from which ships' pursers bought seamen's clothing, and this bulk buying gave a semblance of uniformity. The figure here is based on a sailor who appears behind a group of naval officers in one of the paintings of the 25th Regiment at Minorca, and to judge by his fur cap with a silver coat-of-arms on the front, he is probably meant to be a member of the admiral's or captain's barge. The petticoat was originally a tarred apron.

156. Great Britain: Midshipman, Royal Navy

Midshipmen were given an all-purpose blue and white uniform in 1748, but it was not until about 1758 that the traditional white collar patch with button and twist loop first appeared. A list of a midshipman's kit, in 1780, includes jackets, trousers and round hats, as shown here.

157. Great Britain: Seaman, Royal Navy

By the 1760s the traditional grey jackets and red breeches worn by British sailors had given way to blue jackets, with white or striped 'Ticken' trousers. The small triangular 'apple pasty' hat was now changed for a low crowned hat with a narrow brim, decorated with a ribbon.

158. France: Captain, Royal Navy, Full Dress

In October 1756, a Full Dress, consisting of a blue coat with red cuffs, lined with crimson silk and embroidered in gold according to rank, was authorised for naval officers. With this coat, red breeches, waistcoat and stockings were worn. Captains had a second

row of gold 'cable' embroidery round the cuffs, the pockets of the coat and of the waistcoat, and, from about 1762, two epaulettes. The gorget and shoulder sword-belt shown in this figure are taken from a portrait of an officer who also wears the Cross of the Order of St Louis. The Full Dress was extremely expensive and many officers grew old in the service without ever possessing one, but the orders also authorised the wearing of a blue undress coat edged with gold lace.

159. France: Flag-officer, Royal Navy, Full Dress

Flag-officers in the French Navy had two rows of gold 'cable' embroidery down the front of the coat and round the coat and waistcoat pockets, three rows round the cuffs, and a row down the front and back sleeve seams. The Admiral shown here wears the ribbon and Grand Cross of the Order of St Louis.

160. France: Lieutenant, Royal Navy, Full Dress

French naval lieutenants had a single row of embroidery round the coat, cuffs, waistcoat and pockets.

161. France: Seaman, Royal Navy

The dress of sailors in the French navy was in general similar to that of the British and American navies, in that no distinctive uniform features existed at the time.

162. France: Officer, Corps Royal de l'Infanterie de la Marine

An order of 26 December 1774 created a corps of 100 companies of 'naval infantry', into which the men of the eight regiments raised in 1772 were transferred. Fifty companies were based on Brest, thirty on Toulon and twenty on Rochefort. During the American war all these companies were at sea, and 800 were landed from the fleet on 30 September 1781 to operate with Lauzun's legion at Gloucester Point, opposite Yorktown. Each company consisted of a naval lieutenant, two ensigns, and 118 rank and file. When aboard ship the officers were permitted to wear their naval uniforms.

163. France: Bombardier, Corps Royal de l'Infanterie de la Marine

Three companies of bombardiers were formed on 26 December 1774, one company based at Brest, Toulon and Rochefort. Each company was to consist of a senior and junior naval lieutenant, two ensigns, and seventy rank and file. Their duties were generally to supervise naval gunnery, and when serving ashore they acted either as artillerymen or as grenadiers.

164. United States: Aide-de-Camp to a General Officer, 1780

The distinction of rank by sashes and cockades introduced in 1775 lasted until June 1780 when, following representations by General Jedediah Huntington, new regulations for the dress of General officers and the insignia of rank for all officers were issued. Officers, other than General officers, were to wear the uniforms of their corps. Colonels, lieutenant-colonels and majors were to wear two epaulettes, captains one on the right shoulder, and subalterns one on the left. Aides-de-camp wore the uniform of their regiments, unless they were unattached in which case they wore the uniform of their general, with a green feather in the hat. Aides-de-camp to the commander-in-chief wore green and white feathers. Brigade- and sub-inspectors wore blue feathers.

165. United States: Major-General the Marquis of Lafayette

By the orders of June 1780, general officers were to wear blue coats with yellow buttons, lined and faced in buff, with two epaulettes and white or buff 'undercloaths'. Major-generals were to be distinguished by two silver stars on the epaulette strap, and a black and white feather in the hat. Later amendments to the order specified that the major-generals' feather should have the upper part black and the lower part white.

166. United States: Brigadier-General Anthony Wayne

By the order of June, 1780, brigadier-generals were to be distinguished by one silver star on their epaulette straps, and by a white feather in the hat. The commander-in-Chief seems to have worn three stars on his epaulettes and a plain hat without any feather. The adjutant-general and his assistants were to wear red and green hat feathers. The system adopted in 1780 was based on the French system introduced in 1759. The stars on the epaulettes, in particular, were the same as those used by the corresponding grades of French general officer. The black cockade with a white centre was adopted as a reciprocal gesture to the French who, on their arrival at Newport in July 1780, had paid the compliment of mounting a black American cockade over the white cockade of the Bourbons.

Continental Army Dress Regulations of 1779

In September 1778, 20,000 suits of blue and brown uniforms, faced with red, had been received from France, and with this supply Washington managed to clothe his army for the winter of 1778–1779. Early in 1779 he started to make arrangements to do the same for the following winter. In January he submitted a plan for clothing the army to Congress in which he proposed a different colour for each state with the individual regiments within the State line distinguished by various colours and arrangements of facings, rather in the French style. He also suggested that breeches should be abolished altogether in favour of woollen overalls for winter and linen for summer.

In May the Board of War, to whom Congress had passed on Washington's plan, replied with one of their own, which differed in suggesting that all the uniforms (except for those of the waggoners who were to have brown or grey coats) were to be dark blue, with white linings and buttons, to be worn with white waistcoats and breeches. The infantry was to be divided into four groups of States, each with a different facing colour, as follows:

1.	New Hampshire Massachusetts Rhode Island Connecticut	White facings.
2.	New York New Jersey	Buff facings.
3.	Pennsylvania Delaware Maryland Virginia	Red facings.
4.	North Carolina South Carolina Georgia	Blue facings and white laced button-holes.

The Board of War estimated that 88,480 infantry suits, 6,480 artillery suits, 3,088 cavalry suits, and 6,000 for the waggoners needed to be ordered. Washington approved this plan and on 11 June, the Board submitted further details. The uniforms were to be of the same quality as those of the French army, and the coats were to button 'as low as the waistband, the lapels loose to button over and the coats not sloped away so as to be incapable of covering the belly in cold or rainy weather, the fashion of Europe be what it may;' and they were to have 'a piece of cloth neatly sewed on each elbow'. The original scheme was altered by giving the 2nd group of States yellow buttons and buff linings. The regiments within each group were to be distinguished by white hat and cap buttons, except for group 2 who had yellow, with the following State markings: NH, MB, RI, C, NY, NJ, P, D, M, V, NC, SC and G.

The Board of War's requisitions were passed on to the American Minister at Versailles, but the money available could only purchase 10,000 suits and 15,000 stands of arms and accoutrements, much of which did not arrive until late 1780 and during 1781.

Washington published a condensed version of the Board's scheme in a General Order of 2 October 1779, but it is not clear to what extent the Continental army actually wore these new uniforms. They remained in force until December 1782, when the whole of the Continental infantry and cavalry were ordered to dress in blue with red facings. Nevertheless the blue and white uniforms ordered for group 1 were still in use in 1784. The following nine figures show uniforms of the Continental army in accordance with the 1779 regulations.

167. United States: Fifer, New Jersey Regiments

Drummers and fifers were ordered to wear the reversed colours of their groups. Those of the fourth, or southern group, wore blue coats with white lacing.

168. United States: Sergeant, New York Regiments

Sergeants of infantry were to wear silk epaulettes, white for all regiments except those with buff facings, who were to have buff epaulettes.

169. United States: Field Officer, New Hampshire Regiments

170. United States: Corporal, Delaware Regiments

Corporals of all infantry regiments, except those with buff facings, were to wear two white worsted epaulettes.

171. United States: Captain, Pennsylvania Regiments

172. United States: Private, North Carolina Regiments

173. United States: Sergeant, Corps of Continental Artillery

Knox's Brigade of Artillery, which served with the Main army from 1777–1783, consisted of four battalions of twelve companies each, totalling 729 in all ranks. It also had a company of the Regiment of Artillery Artificers, and civilian drivers, attached to it. In 1781 the establishment was changed to nine companies per battalion, totalling 651 all ranks. The uniform shown here is that laid down in the 1779 regulations. Sergeants were to have two yellow silk epaulettes, and corporals two yellow worsted epaulettes.

174. United States: Officer, Corps of Engineers

There were very few qualified engineers in the Continental army, and most of these were volunteers from the French army. In June 1778 the Corps of Sappers and Miners was formed, to assist the engineers, consisting of three companies of four officers and sixty rank and file, mainly drawn from the ranks of the Connecticut and Massachusetts infantry regiments. By the Order of June 1780, officers of the Corps of Engineers and of the Corps of Sappers and Miners were to wear blue coats, with buff facings and red linings, buff waistcoats and breeches, gold buttons and gold epaulettes of their respective ranks.

175. United States: Drummer, Corps of Continental Artillery

There was one drummer to each company in each battalion of artillery. They wore uniforms of the reversed colours of the corps.

THE WAR IN THE SOUTH

Georgia, 1779

In November 1778 Colonel Campbell was sent to Georgia in command of a small force, and by January 1779 had cleared the province of rebels. In July, however, General Benjamin Lincoln marched on Savannah from Charleston, South Carolina, and was joined by a French force of 6,000 transported from the West Indies by the Comte d'Éstaing. On 9 October, in spite of being outnumbered two to one, the garrison of Savannah repulsed the besiegers, d'Éstaing returned to France, and Lincoln to Charleston.

South Carolina, 1780

On 25 December 1779, Clinton, learning of the lifting of the siege of Savannah, embarked on his long-awaited southern campaign, sailing for Charleston with 8,000 men under the command of himself and Cornwallis. On 30 March 1780 the first parallel was opened, on 7 April American reinforcements marched in, and on 8 May the town was summoned to surrender. On 13 May Lincoln surrendered with 6,000 men, the worst American defeat in the entire revolution.

On 29 May Banastre Tarleton with 290 men massacred Buford with 400 men at Waxhaw Creek. Although Washington had despatched the Baron Kalb to South Carolina with 900 reinforcements, Congress appointed Horatio Gates to the command in the south, without consulting him.

In July Clinton returned to New York leaving Cornwallis to pacify South Carolina with 8,000 men. On 16 August Cornwallis with 2,400 men met Gates with 3,000 at Camden and roundly defeated him. Gates fled to Hillsboro, North Carolina, with the remains of his force, after leaving 900 killed, including the Baron Kalb, and 1,000 prisoners.

North Carolina, 1780-1781

In October Cornwallis commenced his march into North Carolina. On 7 October Major Patrick Ferguson, marching on a parallel course through the backcountry with 1,100 men, was defeated and killed at King's Mountain by 1,400 'mountain men' and militia from North Carolina and Virginia. Cornwallis immediately halted his advance and retired to Winnsborough, South Carolina.

In December Nathanial Greene, who had been appointed to the command in the south by Washington and was once more in charge, arrived at Charlotte, North Carolina, and proceeded to split his force to wage a hit-and-run campaign. He sent Morgan, with 600 men towards Cowpens, and Huger with 1,100 south-east towards Cheraw. On 17 January 1781, Tarleton advanced from Winnsborough with 1,150 men and attacked Morgan at Cowpens. He was routed with the loss of 800 against the American's casualties of seventy-two. Cornwallis, already on the move, nevertheless forced Morgan and Greene to retire before him. At the same time Huger turned north to join the main American army at Guildford Courthouse.

Between January and March Cornwallis vainly exhausted his army chasing Greene across the flooded Catawba and Yadkin rivers, finally giving up the chase at the Dan River, where he turned south, followed by Greene. On 15 March Cornwallis with 2,200 turned to attack Greene with 4,500 at Guildford Courthouse, and defeated him despite his loss of 532 to the Americans' 260. Cornwallis retired to the coast at Wilmington, abandoning South Carolina to Greene, who marched south to mop up any British troops left there.

Virginia, 1780-1781

Between December 1780 and May 1781 the British sent two expeditions, the first under the former American general, Arnold, who was later joined and superseded by Phipps, to carry out a series of raids in Virginia. Eventually Phipps and Arnold decided to march south to join Cornwallis.

For his part Cornwallis had elected to march northwards into Virginia. The two met at Petersburg, Virginia, on 30 May, when their combined force totalled 5,700 men.

On 29 April Lafayette, sent by Washington to reinforce Virginia, arrived at Richmond with 3,550 men. Throughout May and June Cornwallis tried to bring Lafayette to battle and led him a dance through eastern Virginia. First Cornwallis forced Lafayette to retire north-west, pursuing him and sending a raiding force westward to Charlotteville, just as 1,000 reinforcements arrived from the north under General Wayne. He immediately turned towards the sea so as to be near the protection of the British fleet. On 4 August Cornwallis occupied Yorktown under the watchful eyes of Lafayette.

Meanwhile Washington and Rochambeau had joined their forces and sent a request to De Grasse in the West Indies for naval aid. On 13 August De Grasse sailed north, and eight days later Washington and Rochambeau marched south. On 30 August De Grasse arrived in the Chesapeake and disembarked 3,000 troops to reinforce Lafayette. On 5–9 September the naval battle of the Capes took place, effectively sealing Cornwallis off from British naval help, and on 14–26 September Rochambeau with 7,000 men and Washington with 9,500 arrived at Williamsburg, closing the trap on Cornwallis. On 19 October 1781, Cornwallis surrendered the garrison of Yorktown, 7,247 strong, just five days before Clinton with 700 reinforcements arrived in the Chesapeake. On learning of the fate of Yorktown Clinton returned to New York and the major military operations of the American revolution came to an end, although peace was not signed until 1783.

American Order of Battle at Yorktown
Commander-in-Chief
General George Washington

Artillery Brigade	*Cavalry*
B.-Gen. Henry Knox	
2nd Continental Artillery (N.Y. and Conn.)	4th Continental Light Dragoons (Pa.)
1st Continental Artillery (V.)	Armand's Legion
4th Continental Artillery (Pa.)	

Detachments

Light Infantry
Mayor-General the Marquis de Lafayette

B.-Gen. Muhlenberg
1st Bn. (Vose)
Eight M.B. Coys.
2nd Bn. (Gimat)
Five Conn.; two M.B.; one R.H.
3rd Bn. (Barber)
Five N.H., N.J., etc.

B.-Gen. Hazen
1st Bn. (Huntington)
Four M.B., Conn.
2nd Bn. (Hamilton)
Two N.Y., two Conn.
3rd Bn. (Laurens)
Four N.H., M.B., Conn.
4th Bn. (Antill)
Hazen's Canadian Regiment

Major-General
Benjamin Lincoln

B.-Gen. James Clinton
1st N.Y. (Van Schaik)
2nd N.Y. (Van Cortlandt)

Col. Elias Dayton
1st and 2nd N.J. (Ogden)
R.I. Regiment (Olney)

Major-General
Baron v. Steuben

B.-Gen. Anthony Wayne
1st Pa. (Stewart)
2nd Pa. (Harmar)
V. Bn. (Gaskins)

B.-Gen. Mordecai Gist
3rd M.B. (Adams)
4th M.B. (Roxburg)

Sappers and Miners

Delaware Recruits

Militia

General Thomas Nelson
Governor of Virginia

B.-Gen. George Weedon
1,500 men
B.-Gen. Edward Stevens
750 men

B.-Gen. Robert Lawson
750 men
Dabney
State Regiment (200)

French Order of Battle at Yorktown

Lieutenant General
Comte de Rochambeau

Artillery
Cavalry
Lauzen's Legion

Brigade Bourbonnois
Regiment Bourbonnois
Regiment Royal Deuxponts
Brigade Agenois
Regiment Agenois
Regiment Gatenois

Brigade Soissonois
Regiment Soissonois
Regiment Saintonge
Regiment Touraine

British Order of Battle at Yorktown

Lieutenant-General
Earl Cornwallis
Artillery
Cavalry
Queen's Rangers (Simcoe)
British Legion (Tarleton)

Light Infantry (Abercrombie)
Lt.-Col. Dundas
43rd
76th
80th

Brigade of Guards (O'Hara)
Lt.-Col. Yorke
17th
23rd
33rd
71st

German troops
1st Anspach-Bayreuth (Voit)
2nd Anspach-Bayreuth (Seybothen)
Hesse-Cassel Erbprinz (Fuchs)
Hesse-Cassel v. Bose   (O'Reilley)
Hesse-Cassel Jägers   (Ewald)
North Carolina Volunteers (Hamilton) (114)
Pioneers (33)

176. United States: Dragoon, 4th Continental Light Dragoons

Originally dressed in red, this regiment was supplied with captured British coats of the 8th and 24th regiments, but deserter descriptions for the period 1780–1782 mention uniform coats of green, faced red. Sent south in 1780 the regiment suffered badly at Camden, after which the rank and file were taken into Colonel Washington's mixed force. In 1781 it was renamed the 4th Legionary Corps, with an establishment of four mounted and two dismounted troops, totalling 455 of all ranks, and was assigned to the Pennsylvania quota. The figure shown here is dressed for dismounted service.

177. United States: Officer, 2nd Continental Light Dragoons

According to the Board of War's plan of June 1779, the Continental Light Dragoons were to have blue coats faced with white. The N.C.O.s, farriers and saddlers were to have blue epaulettes, and blue cloaks with white collars and green stable-jackets were also mentioned. The trumpeters were at first supposed to wear the same as the dragoons, but they were later ordered to wear white faced and lined in blue. In January 1781 the regiment was renamed the 2nd Legionary Corps and was assigned to the Connecticut quota. One of the last regiments to serve in the war, some of its men feature in Trumbull's paintings wearing blue faced with buff, and carrying helmets with light blue turbans and yellow tassels. The metal helmet shown here is of a typically French design.

178. Provincials: Lieutenant-Colonel Banastre Tarleton, British Legion

Formed by Lord Cathcart in 1778 from loyalists of New York, Pennsylvania and New Jersey, the British Legion achieved considerable fame or, in American eyes, notoriety. Until 1779 the Legion was employed on foraging expeditions and patrolling around New York, and was involved in several skirmishes. In 1780 they were sent south, seeing action at Catawba, Waxhaws and Guildford Courthouse. They were badly cut up at Cowpens, and when Yorktown fell, they surrendered to the French at Gloucester. The figure here is based on the celebrated portrait by Sir Joshua Reynolds in the National Gallery, London, confirmed by a portrait of Colonel George Hanger, who also served in the British Legion. The type of head-dress, which was worn by British light dragoons until 1814, was known as a 'Tarleton' helmet even by the French, suggesting that he was its inventor. An M.S. Almanack for the year 1783 compiled by a Hessian officer, Bernhard de Wiederhold, and belonging to the New York Historical Society, describes the uniform of the Legion cavalry as 'Short Round Tight Jacketts, Black Collar and Cuffs', and that of the infantry as a 'Short Coat-Green with same lappel, variety button hole (viz. laced) & Black Cuff & Collar'; mounted figures in the background of Tarleton's portrait show the men's jackets as being similar to the officers', but with white lace. There are, however, indications that the British Legion may have worn white while campaigning in the south.

179. Provincials: Hussar, Queen's Rangers

In January 1778, a troop of thirty cavalrymen was added to the

Queen's Rangers, and shortly after was dressed as hussars. In 1780, three troops of light dragoons were added who, according to Lefferts, wore Tarleton helmets, green jackets, buckskin breeches, and boots, altogether very similar in appearance to the British Legion. The figure here, showing a hussar of the Queen's Rangers in 1780, is based on a set of drawings in the Toronto Central Library made by the Adjutant of the corps, Captain James Murray. The silver crescent on the front of the cap was engraved QUEEN'S RANGERS.

180. United States: Private, Pulaski's Legion Infantry

In March 1778, after a short spell as a commander of the Continental cavalry, Count Pulaski was authorised to raise an independent corps consisting of three troops of cavalry, a company of *chasseurs*, one of grenadiers, two of infantry, and a 'supernumary company', totalling some 268 men. In February 1779 Pulaski's Legion was sent south but was disbanded after Pulaski's death before Savannah in October. The cavalry went to the 1st Light Dragoons, and the infantry to the 1st South Carolina Regiment. Clothing returns for the years 1778–1780 reveal that both the cavalry and infantry of the Legion were issued with cavalry-type helmets and blue coats faced with red. The cavalry, however, seem to have worn more conventional jackets or sleeved waistcoats, buckskin breeches and boots, when on active service.

181. United States: Brigadier-General Charles Tuffin Armand, Marquis de la Rouerie

Armand, an officer of the French army, took over Baron Ottendorf's Independant Company in June 1777, but it was not until a year later that Armand's 'Free and Independant Chasseurs' were given an establishment of three companies of 150 men each. By August of the same year, however, it had only 153 men in all, many of them former Brunswick prisoners. Late in 1778 a troop of light dragoons was added to Armand's corps which now became a legion. Although it saw plenty of action in the southern campaign, its reputation was not of the highest, since it was renowned chiefly for its ill-discipline. Charles Willson Peale's portrait of Armand, on which the figure here is based, shows him wearing the single star of a brigadier-general on the straps of his epaulettes, and the cross of the French Order of St Louis.

182. United States: Trooper, v. Heer's Provost Corps

In May and June 1778, a Provost Corps of sixty-three Light dragoons (including four executioners) under the command of Major v. Heer, was formed to maintain order in the rear of the Main army. Two N.C.O.s and eight troopers were retained by Washington to carry his despatches until 1783, and were thus the last mounted troops of the Continental army.

183. Provincials: Light Infantrymans Queen's Rangers

184. Provincials: Grenadier, Queen's Rangers

185. Provincials: Sergeant of Riflemen, Queen's Rangers

The Queen's Rangers had originally consisted of eight companies of riflemen, one company of grenadiers, and one of light infantry, but in late 1777 a Highland company was added, clothed in Highland dress with green jackets. The uniforms shown here, which date from 1780, are based on Captain Murray's drawings, and show the light infantry and rifles in caps and sleeved waistcoats. The sergeant has extra silver lace round his collar and cuffs. The Queen's Rangers were placed on the regular establishment in 1779 as the 1st American Regiment, and although disbanded at the end of the war, they were reinstated in December 1791 in Canada. Their present descendants are the Queen's York Rangers of Toronto.

186. United States: Private, 3rd North Carolina Regiment, 1778

Raised in April 1776, this regiment served with the Main army until 1779, when it was reorganised and sent south. Little is known about its uniform, but Lefferts shows men of the regiment in hunting shirts and overalls.

187. United States: Officer, 1st South Carolina Regiment

188. United States: Private, 2nd South Carolina Regiment

The 1st and 2nd South Carolina Regiment, together with a regiment of rangers, were raised in June 1775 for service within the state, but were taken into Continental service. They distinguished themselves in the defence of Fort Moultrie on Sullivan Island during the abortive British attack on Charleston. Both regiments were dressed in blue, sometimes described as black, with red facings, and wore the curious cap with a silver crescent badge associated with South Carolina. That of the 1st Regiment bore the Legend ULTIMA RATIO, and that of the 2nd, LIBERTY, or, LIBERTY OR DEATH. A portrait of Colonel Cotesworth Pinckney shows him in this uniform but with a grenadier cap, which is unfortunately not clear enough to reproduce here. A list of rebel forces at Charleston published in the *Pennsylvania Ledger* on 28 April 1778 mentions the '1st Regiment Colonel Cotesworth Pinckney 450 men black dress faced red, chiefly Carolinians', and the '2nd Regiment Colonel Huger, 395, same dress and some white frocks, chiefly old countrymen'. Both regiments were captured at the fall of Charleston in 1780.

189. Provincials: Private, North Carolina Volunteers

Apart from the fact that 114 men of this regiment were part of Cornwallis's force at Yorktown, little is known about its history. The uniform shown here, red with plain blue lapels, is based on Wiederhold's list.

190. Great Britain: Lieutenant John Caldwell, 8th (or the King's) Regiment, in Indian Dress

From 1768 to 1785 the 8th Regiment served in Canada, garrisoning the forts along the St Lawrence and Great Lakes, and taking part in the fierce backcountry fighting. As adjutant, Caldwell was principally employed during the last years of the war 'delivering the King's presents to the Indians and Exchanging with them the War Hatchet and Wampum'. In the painting, from which this figure is taken, he is shown in the Indian dress that he wore while taking a leading part in the Council held at Wakitomiky on 17 January 1780. He is holding in his hand the wampum belt or 'Hatchet' bearing the design of a tomahawk, which the Americans had sent to the Indians to win over their support. British financial policy, the death of the Indian superintendent John Stuart in March 1779, and the attempts of the Americans to secure the neutrality of the southern Indians all conspired to reduce to a minimum the possible aid which the Indians might have given in the southern campaign.

191. Provincials: Sergeant, 3rd Battalion, De Lancey's Brigade

Raised in 1776 among the loyalists of New York State by Oliver De Lancey, this regiment or 'brigade', consisted of three battalions. At first they were dressed in green, but when the Provincial line went into red De Lancey's were given blue facings, with white buttons and lace, arranged in one's, twos, or threes according to the battalion. They appear to have worn caps and woollen overalls, red, blue, or brown, in winter and hats in summer. The wide-brimmed white hat shown here appears in American deserter descriptions, and was typical wear in the southern states.

The Corps of Light Infantry

In the summer of 1777 Washington formed a small corps of light infantry of men selected from the various regiments of the Continental army, and the regiment was so successful that he obtained permission from Congress the following year to organise a light infantry company in every regiment, after the British model. As in the British army these companies were amalgamated when on campaign and eventually the Corps of Light Infantry, a 2,000-strong division, was formed under the command of the Marquis de Lafayette. Lafayette took great pains with the training and appearance of this force, and it soon became the best-trained and equipped division in the army, distinguishing itself at Stony Point and Yorktown. Lafayette at his own expense provided the battalion colours, one of which bore a cannon and the motto ULTIMA RATIO, and another a wreath of laurels joined with a 'civic crown' and the motto NO OTHER. He also provided the swords for the officers and sergeants. The Corps of Light Infantry was recognisable by its red and black plumes.

192. United States: Private, Rhode Island Light Infantry Company

The negro soldier, of what seems to be a Rhode Island company (to judge by the shape of the cap and the badge of an anchor on its front), is based on a sketch by Baron v. Clausen, one of Rochambeau's aides-de-camp.

193. United States: Officer, New York Light Infantry Company

According to the Frenchman Chastellux, the officers of the Corps of Light Infantry carried swords and spontoons, and the subalterns fusils and bayonets. The figure here is based on one appearing in Trumbull's painting of the British surrender at Yorktown. He wears a normal New York officer's uniform, with a light infantry cap, and wings under his epaulettes.

194. United States: Private, Massachusetts Light Infantry Company

Deborah Sampson, a Massachusetts girl, joined the 4th Massachusetts at West Point, posing as a man, and was posted to the light infantry company. The description of her uniform in her biography refers to 'white wings' on the shoulders, and 'cords on the arms and pockets'. The figure here is a reconstruction from this description, with the addition of a light infantry cap of the type shown by Trumbull.

195. France: Aide-de-camp to a General Officer, Full Dress

Rochambeau had six aides-de-camp on his staff, including the future Marshal Berthier, and the other general officers with him had a total of nine, a number which increased during the campaign as more French officers came out to America in search of employment. The dress of the staff of the French army was regulated in December 1756, and was subsequently modified in orders of April 1767 and September, 1775. Aides-de-camp wore the epaulettes of their rank in the army. Their coats had eight embroidered loops down each front, two on each cuff, and three on each pocket flap.

196. France: Lieutenant-General Comte de Rochambeau, Full Dress

The grades of general officer in the French army were as follows: marshal, lieutenant-general, marshal-of-the-camp, and brigadier-general. While marshals-of-the-camp, of whom Rochambeau had no less than three in America, could command forces of all arms, brigadier-generals could only command forces of their own particular arm. In undress the embroidery on the coat was narrower, and white waistcoat and breeches were worn. In this portrait Rochambeau wears the Ribbon and Grand Cross of the Order of St Louis, which he was awarded in 1771.

197. France: War Commissary, Full Dress

The war commissary, who combined the duties of the British or

American adjutant- and quarter-master-generals, handled all matters of supply, transportation and administration. Besides the Chevalier de Tarle, *Commissaire-Ordonnateur*, Rochambeau had a commissary-general, M. Blanchard, who was assisted by two *commisaires ordinaires*.

198. France: Grenadier, Voluntaires Etrangères de la Marine

Armand-Louis de Gontaut-Biron, duc de Lauzun, raised this corps in September 1778. It was supposed to consist of eight legions and a service company, but it appears that only three were in fact formed. Each legion was to consist of a company of grenadiers, one of *chasseurs*, two of fusiliers, and one each of gunners, hussars and work-men. 'Lauzun's Legion', as it was generally called, took part in the capture of Senegal in December 1778, and a detachment served with distinction under Admiral Suffren in the Indies. The Duke himself led a large part of his corps to America with Rochambeau. The legion counted as a foreign corps for over-seas service and was made up largely of Germans, Poles and Irishmen. The orders were given in German and the uniform of the legion was the horizon blue usually associated with German troops in the French Service. The three legions were distinguished by having different collars and shoul-der-straps – the 1st yellow, the 2nd white, and the 3rd red – and the fusiliers wore cocked hats edged with white braid. A crudely executed figure of a *chasseur* on a recruiting poster 1782 suggests that they may have worn metal helmets, with a fur turban, crest and plume, at the time they were in America.

199. France: Hussar, Voluntaires Etrangères de la Marine

Apart from some cavalry which came with de Grasse from the West Indies and which are variously described as 'dragoons' and 'hus-sars', the hussars of Lauzun's Legion were the only French mounted troops in America. They carried out reconnaissance and patrol duties while the French army was marching south to Williamsburg, after which they were concerned in the fighting around Gloucester Point, opposite Yorktown, where on one occasion they routed Tarleton's legion.

200. France: Corporal, Saintonge Infantry Regiment

There is a certain amount of debate as to the exact dress of the French troops serving in North America. Lefferts and others have stated that they all wore uniforms in accord-ance with the regulations of 1779, but current French opinion sug-gests that probably only the troops of Saint-Simon's corps which accompanied De Grasse to the West Indies wore them. Rocham beau's corps, it is thought, must have left too soon to have received the new clothing, and was there-fore wearing that of 1767, which amended the drastic changes of 1763. Figs. 200–205, therefore, are shown in this earlier dress, and Figs. 206–208 in the later. The 1763 regulations introduced the short coat with narrow cuffs, the white waistcoat and breeches, and the cocked hat which were copied from the Prussians by most of the European armies. The infantry regiments were distinguished by their numbered buttons in white or yellow metal, and by various arrangements of buttons and colours of cuffs, lapels and pipings. Fusiliers had their hats bordered with white or yellow lace according to their buttons. Subsequent to 1767 there were various equipment changes, the most drastic of which was the abolition of the waist-belt for the bayonet, which was henceforth worn in a frog attached to the cartouche box-belt. The Saintonge Regiment bore the number '68' on their buttons.

201. France: Officer, Bourbonnois Infantry Regiment

Officers wore similar uniforms to their men but made from better quality materials. Their officer rank was denoted by their gold or silver epaulettes, depending on the colour of their buttons, and their gilt gorgets which bore the arms of France in silver. The arrangement of epaulettes, which was the most sophisticated system of rank markings in existence at the time, was as follows:

Colonel: Two epaulettes with bullion fringes.

Lieutenant-Colonel: One similar epaulette on the left side.

Major: Two epaulettes with twist fringe.

Captain: One similar epaulette on the left side.

Lieutenant: One epaulette on the left side with the strap metal and coloured silk mixed in a lozenge pattern, with metal and silk fringe.

Sub-Lieutenant: The same but in reversed colours, viz., coloured strap with metal lozenge pattern, mixed fringe.

The figure here represents a captain. On his right shoulder he wears a *contre-epaulette* consisting of a strap which matches that of his epaulette. White gaiters were worn in summer, and black in winter or on the march. Officers' waist-belts were gradually superseded by shoulder sword-belts. The 'Union Cockade' was introduced in Newport Rhode Island in July 1780. The Bourbonnois had the number '9' stamped on their buttons.

202. France: Grenadier, Soissonois Infantry Regiment

From 1767 to 1775 many different styles of head-dress were tried out in the French army: large hats, small hats, boiled-leather caps, metal helmets, black leather helmets and bearskin grenadier caps were all eventually abandoned in favour of the felt cocked hat. However, there is evidence that the Soissonois Regiment was still wearing the grenadier caps that were officially abolished in 1779 when they marched through Philadelphia in 1781 on their way to

Williamsburg and Yorktown. Grenadiers, unlike the fusiliers retained their hangers and therefore wore a second cross-belt from which it hung. The figure here carries the typically French gourd-shaped water-bottle which was worn right through the Napoleonic Wars. The Soissonois Regiment bore the number '23' on their buttons.

203. France: Gunner, Corps Royal de l'Artillerie

In 1767 the French Royal Artillery was numbered '47' in the list of infantry regiments. The distinctions for N.C.O.s were in either gold or yellow worsted braid. The twenty-four senior gunners, bombardiers, sappers, or artificers wore two yellow chevrons, points down, on the left upper arm, and the next twenty-four senior, a single chevron. In 1772 the uniform of the artillery was changed by altering the strip of cloth down the coat fronts, to blue lapels piped in red. The number on the buttons was changed from '47' to '64' at the same time.

204. France: Officer, Corps of Engineers

The Corps of Engineers, formed of Royal Engineer officers, was at one time part of the artillery, but after 1759, it became a separate unit with its own school at Mezières. The officer here wears the later 1772 uniform with the two epaulettes and the bullion fringe of a colonel.

205. France: Officer of Grenadiers, Royal Deux-Ponts Infantry Regiment

This regiment, numbered '92' in the French Line, was raised by the duc de Deux-Ponts (Zweibrucken) on his estates, by a commission dated 1 April 1757. It acquired a reputation for extraordinary bravery, and is said to have led the storming party into Yorktown. Each German regiment in French service favoured a different blue, the Deux-Ponts wearing the sky-blue dear to Bavaria, and it took all St Germain's power to impose a uniform turquoise blue on them all. Officers of grenadiers wore caps like their men with silk cords and tassels, epaulettes and gorgets, and were armed with fusils and bayonets. The regulations of 1776 reduced the number of fusilier companies in the infantry regiment to four per battalion, with a grenadier company with the 1st Battalion, and a *chasseur* company with the 2nd Battalion.

206. France: Sergeant of Chasseurs, Agenois Infantry Regiment

The chief changes brought about by the 1779 dress regulations, illustrated in this and the following two figures, were the regularising of the system for denoting regiments by groups of colours, and revised differences of dress between the grenadier, *chasseur*, and fusilier companies of a regiment. The arrangement of facings within groups has already been described in the introductory section on the

French army. After 1779 *chasseurs* were distinguished by their green shoulder-straps, which were piped in white, and the green cloth bugle horns sewn on the turnbacks of their skirts. Sergeants wore one row of silver braid round the tops of their cuffs. The Agenois Regiment was numbered '16' in 1779.

207. France. Officer Gatenois Infantry Regiment

As before the distinguishing marks of officers were their epaulettes and gorgets. Fusilier companies were denoted by their white shoulder-straps piped in the regimental colour, and the cloth *fleur-de-lis* sewn on the turnbacks, also in the distinguishing colour. Portraits of officers sometimes show them wearing black breeches, which must have been more practical than the white. The Gatenois Regiment was numbered '18' in 1779.

208. France: Grenadier, Touraine Infantry Regiment

The 1779 regulations stipulated a cocked hat for the grenadiers in place of the bearskin cap, but they were to be distinguished by a red pom-pom over the white (or in this case 'union') cockade. They were further distinguished by their red shoulder-straps, piped in white, and the red cloth grenades sewn to their turnbacks. The grenadiers also retained the second cross-belt for their hanger. The Touraine Regiment was numbered '34', in 1779.

American Flags and Colours

The American national flag appeared in two versions: that raised at Cambridge in July 1775 consisted of the 'Union Jack' in the upper canton, and the rest of the flag divided into seven red and six white horizontal stripes. In June 1777 the design of the canton was changed to a dark blue field with thirteen white stars arranged in a circle.

As far as regimental colours were concerned, Major-General Charles Lee seems to have invented a system of one regimental standard and two or four 'grand division' colours per battalion, (a grand division consisting of two companies), before the outbreak of the revolution, and for the rest of the war the Americans wavered between this system, and the two colour system used by the British. In 1776 the regiments of the Continental army were required to have a regimental colour and a grand division colour. A list of colours dating from 1778, unfortunately not attributed to regiments, reveals a system of one regimental colour with one of thirteen distinctive devices and the thirteen stars in the canton, and two plain grand division colours, which were probably painted with the regiment's name and number after being issued. The colours used in this system were green, red, blue or yellow. In 1779, v. Steuben's regulations restored the two-colour system. Each regiment was to have a standard of the United States on a dark blue field, and a regimental colour on a crimson, dark blue, white or buff field, depending upon the facing colour of the regiment. In spite of these rules, however, the three-colour system, with stripes in the upper canton instead of stars, was still in use in some regiments in 1780.

209. Rhode Island Train of Artillery, 1775

210. 1st Continental Regiment, 1776

211. 2nd New Hampshire Regiment, 1777
In the ribbon the motto THE GLORY NOT THE PREY.

212. 2nd New Hampshire Regiment, 1777
The names of the thirteen states on the entwined circles, and the motto WE ARE ONE in the centre.

Both the New Hampshire Regiment colours were captured by the British at Fort Anne, in 1777.

213. 3rd New York Regiment

214. Regimental Colour, Continental Army, 1778
This colour, based on the 'Headman Flag' in the Museum of History and Technology, Washington D.C. and reputed to have been carried at Trenton and Germantown, conforms exactly with one of the Continental colours listed in 1778.

British and Provincial Regimental Colours

The 1768 warrant laid down that the 'King's, or First Colour' of every infantry regiment was to be 'the Great Union throughout'. The second colour was to be the colour of the regimental facings, with the union in the upper canton. Regiments with red or white facings were to have the red cross of St George throughout, with the union in the upper canton, and those with black facings the cross of St George throughout, with the union in the upper canton and the other three cantons black. In the centre of each colour there was to be painted or embroidered in 'Gold Roman characters, the Number of the Rank of the Regiment with a wreath of Roses and Thistles'. Regiments who had 'Royal Devices' or 'Ancient Badges' were permitted to bear them on their colours. The British colours were to be 6 ft 6 ins (2 m) flying, and 6 ft (1 m 85 cm) deep on the pike, which was to be 9 ft 10 ins (3 m) high.

Apart from fluttering bravely at the heads of regiments, the colours served several useful purposes. They marked the position of the regiment in the field, provided a rallying point and, when several regiments were formed in line, could be used to dress the line, each man looking from colour to colour to get his alignment.

215. Regimental Colour, 3rd Regiment

218. Regimental Colour, 23rd Royal Welch Fusiliers

216. King's Colour, 5th Regiment

219. Regimental Colour, 27th or Inniskilling Regiment

217. Regimental Colour, 9th Regiment

220. Regimental Colour, Queen's Rangers

German Regimental Colours

The German regiments, for the most part, had two colours each. In the Hesse-Cassel service the colours of the 'flames' and the field varied without any apparent system, while in the Brunswick service, the colours of the 1st and 2nd colours were reversed. The 1st colour of the Hesse-Hanau Erbinz Regiment bore the full arms of Hesse-Hanau on a pink field. The field of the Anspach-Bayreuth colour was white damask.

221. Hesse-Cassel Fusilier Regiment v. Ditfurth, 1st Colour

saved at Saratoga by Madame v. Riedesel.

222. Hesse-Cassel Musketeer Regiment v. Mirbach, 2nd Colour

225. 2nd Colour, Hesse-Hanau Erbprinz Regiment

223. Brunswick Infantry Regiment Prinz Friedrich, 1st Colour

224. Brunswick Infantry Regiment v. Riedesel, 1st Colour
The colours of this regiment were

226. Anspach-Bayreuth, Infantry Regiment
The reverse of this colour bore the red eagle with ribbon and motto PRO PRINCIPE ET PATRIA.

French Regimental Colours

In the French infantry regiments a single colour, that of the colonel, was entirely white. It was not a royal flag, and its French nationality was proclaimed by the bow or *cravate* of white attached to the pike head. It is said that this bow was introduced to mark out the French flags from those of her enemies in action. The senior ensign carried this white colonel's flag, and the 2nd ensign the 1st *Drapeau d'Ordonnance*, which was that of the lieutenant-colonel's company. There were fourteen other *Drapeaux* to each regiment.

227. 'Drapeaux d'Ordonnance', Bourbonnois Infantry

228. 'Drapeau d'Ordonnance', Touraine Infantry

229. 'Drapeau d'Ordonnance', Soissonois Infantry

230. 'Drapeau d'Ordonnance', Royal Artillerie

231. 'Drapeau d'Ordonnance', Saintonge Infantry

232. 'Drapeau d'Ordonnance', Royal Deux-Ponts Infantry

Firearms

233. British Short Land Pattern smoothbore flintlock, known as 'Brown Bess'

234. Detail of lock (see 233 above)

235. United States 'Committee of Safety' smoothbore flintlock

236. French 1763 Model smoothbore flintlock

237. Detail of lock (see 236 above)

238. French 1777 Model cavalry 'Mousqueton'.

239. United States 'Kentucky Rifle'

240. German Jägerbusche Rifle

Swords and Edged Weapons

241. British officer's smallsword

242. British light infantry smallsword

243. British infantry hanger

244. United States sabre

245. United States smallsword

246. United States hunting sword

247. French grenadier's hanger

248. Brunswick dragoon broadsword

249. Pipe tomahawk

250. Spontoon head

Head-dress

251. British helmet, 17th Light Dragoons

252. United States light dragoon helmet, based on the French model

253. Hesse-Cassel grenadier cap, Regiment v. Rall

254. United States light dragoon helmet, Armand's Legion

255. British grenadier cap

256. Hesse-Cassel fusilier cap, Regiment v. Lossberg

257. United States: Button, 1st Maryland Battalion

258. United States: Button, Rhode Island Regiment

259. United States: Button, Continental Army, after 1778

260. United States: Button, 8th Massachusetts Regiment

261. United States: Delaware Regiment

262. United States: Button, Continental Artillery

263. United States: Button, New Jersey Regiment

264. France: Button, Touraine Infantry Regiment, 1767
French buttons were either yellow or white depending on the regiment

265. Great Britain: Coldstream Guards rank and file
In the British infantry all the rank and file buttons were white. The buttons of the officers were either gold or silver depending on their lace.

266. Brunswick: Cartouche box plate

267. Hesse-Cassel: Cartouche box plate

268. Provincials: Standard cartouche box plate. The title of the unit was engraved on the circle

269. Provincials: Standard shoulder-belt plate

270. Great Britain: Officers' gorget

271. Shoe buckle

272. Waist buckle of breeches

273. Knee buckle of breeches
N.B. Figs 257–273, above, are not drawn to a constant scale.

British Infantry and Artillery Facings and Rank and File Lace

As each British regiment had its own distinctive facing colour and pattern of lace, we have felt that it would be useful to include here this information for all the British regiments serving in North America during the war. The lace has been arranged in a typical button-hole loop.

274. Coldstream Guards, worn in pairs

275. 3rd Foot Guards, worn in threes

276. 3rd Regiment, or the Buffs

277. 4th, or the King's Own Regiment

278. 6th Regiment

279. 7th, or Royal Fusiliers

280. 8th, or King's Regiment

281. 9th Regiment

282. 10th Regiment

283. 14th Regiment

284. 15th Regiment

285. 16th Regiment

286. 17th Regiment

287. 18th, or Royal Irish

288. 19th Regiment

289. 20th Regiment

290. 21st, or Royal North-British Fusiliers

291. 23rd, or Royal Welch Fusiliers

292. 24th Regiment

293. 26th Regiment

294. 27th, or Inniskilling Regiment

295. 28th Regiment

296. 31st Regiment

297. 34th Regiment, worn in pairs

298. 35th Regiment

299. 37th Regiment

300. 40th Regiment

301. 43rd Regiment

302. 44th Regiment

303. 46th Regiment

304. 47th Regiment

305. 50th Regiment, worn in pairs

306. 52nd Regiment

307. 53rd Regiment

308. 54th Regiment

309. 55th Regiment

310. 56th Regiment

311. 59th Regiment

312. 60th, or Royal Americans

313. 62nd Regiment

314. 63rd Regiment

315. 64th Regiment

316. 65th Regiment

317. 70th Regiment

318. 71st Highland Regiment (Fraser's)

319. 74th Regiment

320. 76th Highlanders (Macdonald's)

321. 80th, or Royal Edinburgh Volunteers

322. 82nd Regiment

323. 84th, or Royal Highland Emigrants

324. Royal Regiment of Artillery

325. First Regiment of Foot Guards

326. 5th Regiment

327. 22nd Regiment, worn in pairs

328. 29th Regiment

329. 30th Regiment

330. 33rd Regiment

331. 38th Regiment

332. 42nd, or Royal Highlanders

333. 45th Regiment

334. 49th Regiment

Bibliography

Certain periodicals have been indispensable in writing this book, in particular the *Military Collector and Historian*, and the *Journal of the Society for Army Historical Research*. It would be impossible to list all the articles consulted individually, but I would particularly like to acknowledge the valuable contribution made by the articles of the following historians and artists: Anne S. K. Brown, Albert W. Haarmann, Herbert Knötel, Colonel Harry C. Larter Jnr, Eugene Leliepvre, Charles McBarron Jnr, Harold Peterson and Frederick P. Todd. The main works consulted are listed below.

BALCH, THOMAS. *The French in America*. Porter & Coates, London (1891).

BAUERMEISTER, ADJUTANT-GENERAL CARL. *Revolution in America*. Rutgers University Press, New Brunswick, U.S.A. (1957).

BELCHER, HENRY. *The First American Civil War, First Period, 1775–1778*. Macmillan & Co., London (1911).

BERG, FRED ANDERSON. *Encyclopaedia of Continental Army Units*. Stackpole Books, Harrisburg, U.S.A. (1972).

BISHOP, MORRIS. 'The End of The Iroquois', *American Heritage*, Vol. XX, No. 6. October 1969.

BOTTET, MAURICE. *Monographies de l'Arme Blanche (1789–1870), et de l'Arme à Feu Portative (1718–1900)*. Editions Haussman (1959).

CURTIS, EDWARD E. *The Organization of the British Army in the American Revolution*. E.P. Publishing Ltd., Wakefield, England (1926).

DUPUY, ERNEST R. AND TREVOR N. *The Encyclopaedia of Military History*. Macdonald & Co., London (1970).

DURUY, ALBERT. *L'Armée Royale en 1789* (1888).

FIELD, COLONEL CYRIL. *Britain's Sea-Soldiers*. Lyceum Press (1924).

FORTESCUE, HON J. W. *A History of the British Army*, Volume III. Macmillan & Co., London (1911).

GREENE, FRANCIS V. *The United States Army* (no date).

HANGER, COLONEL GEORGE. *The Life, Adventures and Opinions of Colonel George Hanger, written by Himself* (1801).

JARRETT, DUDLEY. *British Naval Dress*. Dent, London (1960).

JOHNSTON, H. P. *The Campaign of 1777 around New York and Brooklyn* (1878).
—— *The Yorktown Campaign and the Surrender of Cornwallis*. Harper Bros., New York, U.S.A. (1881).

JOHNSTON, CHARLES M. *The Valley of the Six Nations*. University of Toronto Press, Canada (1965).

KATCHER, PHILIP. *The American Provincial Corps, 1775–1784*. Osprey Publishing Co., Reading, England (1973).

KLINGER, ROBERT L. AND WILDER, RICHARD A. *Sketch Book 76*, private (1967).

LACHOUQUE, HENRI. *Dix Siècles de Costume Militaire*. Hachette, Paris (1963).

LARTER, COLONEL HARRY C. JNR. 'German Troops with Burgoyne, 1776–1777', *The Bulletin of the Fort Ticonderoga Museum (North American Review)*. Volume IX (1952).

LAWSON, C. C. P. L. *A History of the Uniforms of The British Army. Volume III.* Norman Military Publications, London (1961).

LEFFERTS, LIEUTENANT CHARLES M. *Uniforms of the American, British, French, and German Armies in the War of the American Revolution, 1775–1783* (1926). Republished We Inc., Connecticut, U.S.A. (1971).

MANGERAND, J. *Armement et Equipement De L'Infanterie Française Du XVIe au XXe Siècle*. Les Editions Militaires Illustrés (1945).

Neptunia, Revue De L'Association Des Amis Du Musée De La Marine.

Le Passepoil, Bulletin Illustre de La Societé d'Etude Des Uniformes.

PEARSON, MICHAEL. *Those Damned Rebels*. Heinemann, London (1972).

PETERSON, HAROLD L. *The Book of the Continental Soldier*. Stackpole Books, Harrisburg. U.S.A. (1968).

RANKIN, COLONEL ROBERT H. *Uniforms of the Sea Services*. United States Naval Institute (1962).

REVOL, COLONEL J. *Histoire De l'Armée Française*. Libraire Larousse, Paris (1929).

REYNOLDS, P. W. *Military Costume of the 18th and 19th Centuries* (MS).

ROGERS, COLONEL H. C. B. *Weapons of the British Soldier* (1960).

ROSCOE, THEODORE AND FREEMAN, FRED. *Picture History of the U.S. Navy*. Charles Scribners Sons, New York, U.S.A. (1956).

RUSSEL, FRANCIS. 'Father of the Six Nations'. *American Heritage*, Volume X, No. 3. April 1959.

Carnet de la Sabretache

SCHOOLCRAFT, HENRY R. *Notes on the Iroquois*. Bartlett & Welford (1846).

——*History of the Indian Tribes of the United States*. J. B. Lippincott & Co., Philadelphia, U.S.A. (1857).

SMITH, PAUL H. *Loyalists and Redcoats*. Chapel Hill, University of North Carolina Press, U.S.A. (1965).

TELFER DUNBAR, JOHN. *History of Highland Dress*. Oliver & Boyd, Edinburgh (1962).

THOUMAS, GENERAL. *Les Anciennes Armées Françaises*. H. Lauriette & Cie (1890).

Tradition

WEELAN, JEAN-EDMOND (Lawrence, Lee, Tr.). *Rochambeau Father and Son*. Henry Holt & Co., New York, U.S.A. (1936).

WILBUR, C. KEITH. *Picture Book of the Continental Soldier*. Stackpole Books, Harrisburg, U.S.A. (1969).

WRIGHT, COLONEL JOHN WOMACK. *Some Notes on the Continental Army* (1963).

Zeitschrift fur Heeres-und Uniformkunde.